AMERICA'S FUTURE:
REQUIEM OR RENAISSANCE?

*An Agenda for the Transformation
of Our Nation and Ourselves*

Bernard Gluckstern

RoseDog Books

PITTSBURGH, PENNSYLVANIA 15238

RoseDog Books
585 Alpha Drive
Suite 103
Pittsburgh, PA 15238
Visit our website at *www.rosedogbookstore.com*

ISBN: 978-1-4809-6377-1
eISBN: 978-1-4809-6399-3

CONTENTS

Preface   v

Introduction   1

1. The Techniques and Technologies of Ensuring a Compliant Nation   31

2. The Psychopathology in which these Elites are Imprisoned and the Inimical Results of Its Expression   69

3. Creating and Implementing the Moral and Economic Foundations of an American Future that Is Equitable   83

4. A Prospective Course of Individual Action that both Maximizes Your Human Potential and Happiness, and Liberates this Nation from Our Collective Impotence and Impoverishment   107

5. Two Standards of Moral Measurement to both Define Exemplary Commercial Enterprises and Identify Those Corporate Culprits Whose Manifold Realities are Among the Most Reprehensible   113

PREFACE

This manuscript is the culmination of a life's experiences devoted to an exploration of the human condition. The content of these events is numerous in character and substance. It is derived from an unceasing inquiry into the meaning of theological systems, spiritual principles, various clinical musings, and therapeutic processes. It is the result of investigations into the historical and contemporary perspectives of those who embrace a Humanist philosophy. In addition, elements of an existential lexicon and political and social theorists, who have also located their normative moorings within this realm, are included.

The vantage point from which I promulgate this document is my personal empirical journey from birth to the current time frame in which I have attained the status of senior citizen. At its epicenter, my existence is comprised of accomplishment and failure, passion and periods of ennui, soaring emotional and intellectual epiphanies, and intractable episodes of obtuseness and self-destructive behavior. Moreover, this is a tale of the acquisition of material affluence and a subsequent period during which I squandered this wealth as well as incidents in which arrogance, self-aggrandizement, and exaggerated achievements appear in this recounting. But perhaps the most regrettable constellation of behavioral misdeeds for which I have been occasionally responsible are cruelty, abusiveness, and a massive and impregnable self-absorption. Thus, it is a life in many respects that mirrors common human frailties if not in quantitative terms certainly in the fact these actions and emotional states may have composed a portion of your personal narrative.

Although the further development of this treatise may occasionally make reference to those events which have in some fundamental regard shaped my code of ethics or revised my moral assessments, you should not construe this to be primarily a memoir or an autobiography. Rather, it is my fervent hope what emerges here will be through the amalgam of scholarship and the content of my experience; a valuable contribution to the dialogue and activities which attracted ever greater consideration in the Spring of 2015.

At the center of frenetic dialogue is an effort to formulate a response to the question:

> *How may we, as individuals and as a society, alter the trajectory of our current path, and thus, avoid the dire consequences to our nation that remaining on this course will ensure?*

To respond to the preceding interrogatory, it is imperative I present to the reader the strategic and tactical dimensions of what is required to achieve this transformation of our nation and our populace. In addition, the principal components and normative environment I am advocating as optimal replacements for our current cultural/institutional arrangements are needed as well. Though it is my intent to delineate in much greater detail the paradigm I am recommending, permit me to provide at this juncture a general frame of reference to those values and dynamics that provide the shape to this alternative social vision.

At the heart of this undertaking is the trinity of concepts of ethical considerations, equitable cultural institutions, and a vibrant and dynamic self-transcendence that must become robust and thriving social realities for the rescue of this culture to become feasible. In my view, they reside at the epicenter of those imperative qualities crucially absent in both our national conversation and, more tragically, in our contemporary civilization.

Beyond all else, this undertaking is dedicated to the identification and presentation of that body of evolving insight and innovation that has begun the process of both resuscitating the American dream and providing a normative and institutional framework that will supplement and supplant our current national status of decomposition, conflict, and divisiveness. It shall also retard the deterioration of what was once a robust, expanding, and dominant consensus of our citizens about our social purpose and our raison d'etre. Thus, this is a continuing search for transformative cultural insight and social wisdom.

These immutable truths cannot be found in any ideology or vapid self-confirming media platforms, which do nothing but reinforce our prejudices and invigorate our smug self-assurances about the nature of our lives and world. Nor can it be glimpsed in provocative sound bites or invidious pronouncements reflecting ethnic prejudices and repugnant social stereotypes. It most certainly is not present in diatribes that embrace warring paradigms, venomous and disrespectful dialogue, and the attempt by so many to contemptuously demonize as enemies those with whom they are in substantial disagreement. Rather, it can be detected within both the theologies of the ancient and the more contemporary assertions of those who embrace the central tenets of the philosophical system of Humanism, and that aspect of existential epistemology which embraces the teleological dynamic.

In these realms, whether the source is a prophetic Judaism or the Christian gospels, the revelations of Mohammed at the center of an Islamic consciousness or the assertions of primary texts within Buddhism, and in sacred

Hindu pronouncements can this normative predicate be discovered. These foundational principles may also be detected in other sources which are secular in character such as Aristotelian and Kantian epistemological prescriptions and within the optimistic life-affirming existentialism of Camus. Through these we unearth a commonalty of vision and moral definition that speaks to the most imperative requirement of all civilizations.

The crucial necessity is to regard both the individual human life and the collectivity of mankind as inviolate entities and sentient beings of unparalleled intrinsic value that, by their very existence, require the society in which they dwell to provide a foundation of ethical principles reflected in those daily realities of which this culture is composed. From these three points of consideration (i.e. major religious traditions and Humanistic and Existentialist philosophic moral frameworks), other moral imperatives will flow. Among them is the obligation to view human beings as inherently deserving of unabridged respect and personal sovereignty, as innately capable of contributions to our collective welfare, and inherently worthy recipients of life-sustaining material resources from our society.

Therefore, this reality demands, by simple virtue of our human status, environments in which ample opportunities are bestowed to enable these individuals to experience the full richness of an invigorating, dynamic, spiritual, and intellectual consciousness as well as a social atmosphere making provision for the satisfaction of their basic material requirements. Examining contemporary American society through the lens of those moral prerequisites, we discover a civilization that fails abysmally to translate these ethical underpinnings into institutional realities.

In subsequent portions of this literary effort, I shall both completely render the totality of the tragic tapestry of a failing nation as well as the content (i.e. structures and specifics of the alternative model I am proposing). However, prior to the commencement of these tasks a number of critical acknowledgements are required. For in the absence of these individuals whose brilliant and rev-elatory insights, as well as the many decades they have devoted to both de-vising the paradigms, on which I draw, and acting as participants in the implementation of these enlightened social, political, and economic con-structs, the formulation of my agenda would not be possible.

To David Korten, whose continuing efforts at demythologizing multi-national behemoths and the baleful reach and corrosive influence of their activities. I am most appreciative of your efforts.

To Gar Alperovitz, for extending the boundaries of economic democracy and creating those decentralized commercial enterprises, both here and abroad, in which employees are both equity holders and simultaneously in-fluence the strategic direction and operational policies under which they labor. I am indebted to you for your profound creativity.

To David Orr, whose multi-decade initiatives regarding environmental issues and, more recently, within the realm of sustainable social and eco-nomic dynamics, as well as your present attempt to translate these normative concerns into reality beneath the umbrella of the Oberlin Project. I salute your resilience and unceasing exertions.

To Harold Meyerson, whose analysis and trenchant criticism, which fre-quently appears on the Op-Ed page of the Washington Post, regarding the soaring economic inequality in the U.S., and what these inequities augur for the continuing dissolution of our democratic system, I am constantly amazed by the ingenuity of your counsel for ameliorating these horrific realities.

To Marcus Raskin, who has expended enormous cognitive and physical energy to demythologize the political imperatives of the national security state, which have been asserted for decades by its apologists and for envi-sioning the progenitor of many contemporary exertions to transform this nation, i.e. "The Encyclopedia of Social Reconstruction;" you are a na-tional treasure.

To those at the World Watch Foundation, who cast a searing and uncompromised illumination upon the massive transgressions for which numerous corporate entities are culpable, and the unceasing audacious proposals and initiatives you present to attain and perpetuate a "Sustainable Economy and Enlightened Politics." You have my unrestricted respect and admiration.

To Professor Myron K. Sibley of Philosophy at Alfred University (tragically deceased), your classes were extraordinary exercises in both a comprehensive exploration of those crucial normative issues that remain timeless, and the rigor and systematic methods of analysis and evaluation you required of your students to adopt when assessing these epistemologies.

The preceding compilation is a fraction of those individuals who have impacted my life in some truly enormous regard. Both space and time restrictions prevent me from formulating an enumeration that is complete, for that would include dozens of former teachers, associates, and friends who represent all walks of life in this society. Suffice it to say, they have contributed immeasurably to the world view I reflect and the richness and complexity of the existence I have experienced, thus far.

Finally, I must pay tribute to my wife, Lisa, who in the course of our marriage and our prior relationship has been unstinting in her devotion, love, and support for the various projects I have addressed, and most magnanimous and fervent in her passionate encouragement of this particular exercise in scholarship, as well.

Bernard S. Gluckstern

April, 2015

Washington, D.C.

INTRODUCTION

The spring of 2015 has enveloped our nation's capitol in the comforting warmth of escalating temperatures. However, these meteorological facts are not relevant to the mood in Washington and in much of our nation.

Many of our citizens', regardless of their locales, ethnic origins, and employment status or in the statistically significant group of the unemployed and underemployed, i.e. approximately twenty-three million), emotional states are frequently alienated, bewildered, in some instances completely incredulous, and enraged about the current circumstances obtained. Almost all of us are tragically familiar with the litany of those pathologies which have been impacting our country for more than four decades. However, the ferocity and divisiveness which are manifest in the often uncivil, profane, and disrespectful, current interactions among these rabid partisans cause substantial damage to the social fabric of American life.

Arrayed on one perimeter of the U.S. are those who wish, at all costs, to retain the hegemony within our cultural paradigm the ascendancy of the European values of which they are the descendants. In concert with this group are Tea Party members who argue government must reflect, in its policies and programs, an ideological purity and fidelity to ultra-conservative principles.

In addition, this coterie of principally Caucasian citizens, many of whom embrace a fundamentalist Christian perspective and reside in the South, are found to be a sprinkling of racists, anarchists, survivalists, and isolationists who bitterly resent those minorities that comprise recent waves of immigration. Also, they denigrate the evolving influence of women and progressive policies which assist the poor and the struggling middle classes by a paltry redistribution of tax revenues to these individuals.

However, beyond all these objections lies the primary, if unspoken, fear that, ultimately before 2050 in fact, the majority of our citizens will be non-Caucasian, thus imperiling the dominant social status and privileged vantage point, that preponderantly white males have enjoyed since the founding of this nation.

The ranks of these activists are certainly responsible for much of the political venom, protests, and the unprecedented obdurateness of Congressional representatives, both in the House and Senate, who view compromise as a betrayal of their allegiance to their constitutional responsibilities. However, they are not the principal culprits who have created and sustained the climate of rancor, disdain, gridlock, and enmity among those who in previous eras were collegial, respectful, and capable of a pragmatic quid pro quo in the service of discharging their obligations as federal lawmakers. Those who bear the primary onus of what occurs in the political, financial, and social spheres of this culture can be found in the towers of behemoth transnational corporate entities.

In concert with the more than 30,000 lobbyists that blanket this city, they ensure whatever legislation, policies, programs, and regulatory initiatives materialize will allow this miniscule class at the apogee of our social pyramid to retain their fiscal advantages and virtually complete dominion over this nation's economy. This fraction of one percent of our population dominate our electoral processes at the federal and, increasingly, the state level by virtue of their unrestricted capability through PAC's (political action committees) to contribute the funds office seekers require to mount campaigns. Moreover, as the result of a recent Supreme Court determination (Citizens v. United), corporations have succeeded in negating the very modest campaign finance reforms that existed prior to that decision.

At the state level, increased donations from these plutocrats influences the composition of the judiciary and the important decisions they hand down that affect business practices, policies, and the tone and tenor of the regulatory climate that prevails in these locales. Members of the state legislatures who hold important posts among their party's leadership are the recipients of significant corporate largesse, to ensure legislation beneficial to their interests becomes law, and those bills inimical to their concerns and priorities are rejected.

Regarding the Congress, its dysfunction and virtual inaction are of little consequence to those who sit at the apogee of our Fortune 500 corporations for those federal programs enacted and funded, other than those sums appropriated for national defense purposes that are redistributionist in character, are irrelevant to their personal requirements. It is not germane because their enormous wealth allows them the discretion from their individual assets to purchase whatever medical, educational, retirement programs, recreational options, and fleets of luxury automobiles and aircraft with palatial appointments or other indulgences they or their families deem necessary.

The sole area of concern to this minute constituency occurring within the House and the Senate are the laws impacting the credit worthiness of our nation's sovereign currency, and the retention and expansion of those loopholes in the tax code allowing these corporations to reduce their obligations to the IRS.

To ensure this area of congressional and executive branch activity, i.e. legislative and regulatory, their interests are protected, they employ approximately sixty lobbyists, attorneys, accountants, sources of political intelligence, and consulting firms in Washington for each member of Congress. However, the depth and breadth of their influence in this society extends far beyond the mechanisms of government to include virtually every sector and segment of our nation. Through such activities as "Strategic Philanthropy," they provide contributions to those institutes and centers that espouse the validity of their mercantile ascendant ideology, i.e. the operation of "free markets," limited government, reduced taxes, and the innate benevolence and public interested nature of the corporate and financial sectors of our economy.

Universities seeking to enlarge their curriculum to emphasize scientific and technical course offerings are frequently the recipients of their support, while those educational institutions that remain committed to the proposition the central component of any education resides in, the Humanities and Social Sciences, find their proposal spurned and requests rejected. For it is within these disciplines in which the cognitive capacity to objectively examine normative concerns, and the capacity to form critical intellectual capabilities in order to evaluate and select those choices, both for their lives and this society to reinforce those values, that animated this democracy's founding. The financial resources for a curriculum of the reaffirmation of those concepts of educational opportunity for all, social and economic mobility to those who are competent and industrious, and a system of government responsive to the concerns of the majority of our citizens, are frequently withheld by these plutocrats.

Beyond our borders, these entities engage in commercial contractual relationships with despots and other anti-democratic political systems to acquire access to such natural resources as oil and gas, gold, diamonds, copper, and other precious materials. These financial arrangements enrich the elites of these societies, but rarely benefit the vast majority of the populations who live in squalor and illiteracy, and are bereft of healthcare, electricity, and are involuntary residents in a state of intractable and grinding poverty.

Our economy's continued immersion in arcane, complex, and speculative financial transactions that reflect substantial risk to our society augurs the possible recurrence of the extraordinary damages and suffering which the Great Recession inflicted upon our citizens.

However, totally oblivious to these risks, senior executives at investment banking firms and hedge funds continue to derive millions of dollars, annually, as their compensation for producing income streams that primarily enrich our nation's community of billionaires. In addition, in the realm of the print and electronic media, huge conglomerates continue to acquire various publications and television and radio stations of significant regional, national, and international reputation. Once they are safely nestled in their portfolios, they ensure their editorial policies, op-ed commentators, and stable of reporters reflect a general adherence to those views and perspectives often respectful and supportive of the contemporary structure of American life, i.e. capitalism, limited government, and taxation policies which benefit the wealthy. This consolidation significantly reduces the spectrum of opinion and debate which these entities previously championed, and thus narrows the limits of dialogue and discussion that fall within "acceptable parameters" of consideration, as possible political solutions to our contemporary difficulties.

Moreover, political candidates, whether they stand for office in municipal, state, or federal elections, are subject to a similar litmus test regarding the matter of campaign contributions. Those who advocate for reforms of current laws or seek to introduce new legislation, policies, programs, or institutional innovations, which are inimical to the interest of this class, will be snubbed and their opponents, who fundamentally advocate on behalf of the status quo, will be rewarded. With regard to the impact which their priorities exert beyond the World Trade Organization and the G-8 or G-20 institutions, as well as NAFTA's continuing mode of operation, their influence is also a dominant factor in the content of other trade pacts currently being negotiated among the U.S., Canada, and Mexico, the U.S. and Japan, and the U.S. and Korea.

Moreover, recent intensified involvements of these companies have been observed in both supporting financially the activities of various U.N. commissions and agencies, and serving as official and ex-officio members of these bodies that shape and construct the result of these research and policy deliberations to ensure their interests are protected. However, the sector of commercial activity most pernicious and irrevocably damaging to our country are the activities of the most efficacious and affluent of U.S. corporations and their foreign cohorts, the energy conglomerates.

In some fundamental regard, the ninety members in this segment of the global economy wield greater influence than sovereign governments and all international organizations, both individually and collectively. Their strategic objectives reflect the central desire to create in all nations and areas of this world an insatiable appetite for the consumption of energy, whether it is the construction of massive infrastructure projects such as roads and dams or the consequent electrification of cities and rural regions of the developing world. Their principal goal is to stimulate the manufacture of trucks and automobiles, as well as the burgeoning distribution of computers mobile phone towers, radio and television stations, and the pervasive use of advertising venues that consume enormous quantities of energy, to illuminate the beguiling messagess these billboards incessantly reiterate. In addition, their intense wish is to increase the dynamic of globalization and continually elevate the international exchange of goods and agricultural produce that finds its way around the globe, on huge container ships and oil tankers that consume during their journeys substantial energy resources.

Recently, as the result of the discovery of substantial natural gas deposits throughout our northeast, plains states, and other areas of this nation, these companies have begun to drill thousands of new wells. They are constructing huge interstate pipelines and facilities for refining and transporting this energy source to Europe, China, and other global destinations. Frequently in their public statements and within their advertising campaigns, their CEO's often refer to their patriotic impulses to reduce our nation's dependence on foreign sources of energy, which these domestic deposits once extracted will achieve. Yet, when inquiries about the damage to crucial underground water tables, which the process of extracting this gas requires, i.e. "fracking," they dismiss the concerns of epidemiologists and numerous citizen groups whose empirical data document the dangers to our health, which the use of these toxic chemicals produces. They categorize the perspectives of these groups as the unfounded rants of those who wish to obstruct the desire of these corporations to profit from both the greatly expanded use of natural gas domestically and the global market's appetite for this source of energy. Moreover, they proudly proclaim the price for this product is much less expensive than the price of a barrel of oil, which presently hovers around a sixty dollars a barrel, on the various national and international commodity exchanges.

Thus, as has been the reality historically, these entities, in the service of fraudulent patriotic motives and concurrent profitability considerations, can justify their enormous damage to our environment and our most precious natural resource, our supplies of potable water.

A candid enumeration of all those inimical activities for which multi-national corporations are responsible could consume numerous chapters of this document. To cite additional examples of their misdeeds, however, would be a superfluous exercise in scholarship, in my view. Should the reader wish a fuller enunciation of the behaviors of rapaciousness, greed, and the concomitant diminishment of our civic culture and the emasculation of our democratic processes, I commend you to David Korten's masterpiece, "When Corporations Rule the World."

However, in my view, in order to fully comprehend both the intrinsic essence and the central dynamics of these entities, it is necessary to address both their status as organic persons, which the courts have conferred upon these institutions historically, and the fundamental goals and concerns that animate these corporations. Beyond all else mammoth public companies in the U.S. are dedicated to a trinity of objectives, all three of which relate exclusively to the fiscal health and well-being of their shareholders and most senior executives.

Their principal obsession is the matter of the value of their equity shares which are listed and trade on such exchanges domestically as the New York Stock Exchange and NASDAQ. In order to attract continuing investment capital for their purchase, it is imperative the quarterly reports which they submit to the SEC continue to reflect the maximum revenues and profitability targets which their financial public relations units had previously forecast, which is the second element of their great concern.

The final component of their obsession is the matter of ensuring, through various committees of the Board of Directors, their salaries, stock incentives, and bonuses are retained at the current exponential levels, which in some instances, exceed a 300 multiple of the wages of their average employee. Moreover, these compensation packages are frequently provided whether or not the previous forecasts are achieved or not, and are awarded in situations in which the fortunes of the company decline, either in relative terms to previous years or in some absolute sense, when in fact the company does not reflect any profit whatsoever and sustains substantial losses.

All other considerations are secondary and perhaps tertiary in importance. If externalities of their operations impact negatively on the environment, as so many energy companies do, the funds provided are anemic and wholly insufficient to address a mitigation of these damages, if allocated at all. From a corporate perspective, it is the responsibility of the federal government to ameliorate the negative consequences in those instances in which toxic waste has been disposed of in the oceans, lakes, streams, or buried in shallow graves and dump sites for the hazardous waste materials their manufacturing processes often produce in substantial quantity.

Other internal funding priorities, which are casualties of senior management's desire to maximize price per share, dividends, profitability, and maintain stratospheric compensations levels for they and their colleagues, are research and development efforts, and allocating disproportionately the productivity gains their employees have achieved, to the fiscal categories cited above. Moreover, the wage increases awarded to their average employee provides a new and emaciated meaning to the term "paltry," if any. There isn't any interest in increasing productive capacity within their manufacturing facilities, or funneling resources into technological support systems, or personnel training. But perhaps the most egregious sins of which these corporations are guilty is abandoning their status as U.S. corporations and relocating through various merger opportunities with foreign companies in order to reduce their tax burdens, and by so doing deprive the federal government of those billions of dollars which they had previously provided.

A related tactic is to accumulate trillions of dollars in overseas bank accounts they refuse to repatriate due to the tax obligations their transfer to domestically situated U.S. banks would require. In addition, their armies of lobbyists have persuaded Congress to implement various tax exemptions, which have reduced their revenue obligations to our nation. As a result of these continuing efforts, these entities have accelerated the transfer of their financial burdens from the corporate and financial sectors of our economy to this nation's middleclass. This evasion of responsibility extends beyond the corporate environment to numerous individual plutocrats who deposit their enormous personal wealth in such tax havens as Panama, the Isle of Jersey, Switzerland, Luxembourg, etc. where insular privacy laws protect them from the prying eyes and inquiries of American investigators. Their behavior enriches a most narrow sliver of our populace while simultaneously reflecting a malevolent indifference to the deterioration of so many social institutions and political processes.

As these entities become ever more impotent and incapable of influencing the nation's direction and future, do these realities augur a national destiny of increased economic hardship for the masses, and the concomitant unrest and conflict which these conditions shall produce.

Whatever historical benefits corporate capitalism has produced in past eras of our nation's history, it has become abundantly clear the modus operandi of these commercial enterprises has created such inequality among our citizens and the continuing erosion of the political efficacy of a vast majority of our population, is no longer viable. This judgment is derived from both a humanist's ethical vantage point and from the content of the moral imperatives, which both the Judeo-Christian principles infused in our founding beliefs and our contemporary commitments to all of those who are citizens of this nation.

Prior to the current era of transnational corporate structures, our nation's entrepreneurial spirit fostered the creation of hundreds of thousands of commercial enterprises, as those with a desire to provide both products and services to an expanding nation and control their economic destinies, became the founders of these business ventures. Beyond their establishment, these merchants devoted, through assiduous and unceasing effort, responsiveness to evolving market circumstances required to ensure their growth and profitability.

Concomitant with these activities did a minute number of industrialists emerge to manufacture steel and create a national network of both the telegraph, and passenger and commercial rail systems. Their ceaseless geological exploration unearthed mammoth oil and gas deposits in many areas of the country, which provided the sources of energy to accelerate the introduction of electrification within urban areas and rural expanses of the U.S. Bankers, such as Chase and Morgan in the east and such entities as Wells Fargo and Bank of America in the west, began the process of expansion with a burgeoning presence initially within the states of their establishment. As they evolved, they became regional entities in the scope of their banking activity and ultimately, through mergers and acquisitions, had become by the final quarter of the twentieth century, financial institutions with a national reach and impact.

From these accomplishments and the influence their political contributions obtained from federal regulators and the enactment of Congressional legislation favorable to their corporate strategic objectives they meticulously constructed the foundation of an international monetary system under their dominion, which was truly global, by the advent of the twenty-first century.

In the realm of agriculture and textiles, and pork and beef production, as well as timber and tobacco in the South and Southwest, and furniture manufacturing facilities and cotton production in the Southeast; all grew exponentially.

As American ingenuity gave birth to such inventions as the telephone, motion pictures, radio and ultimately television, and the introduction of mass production techniques to manufacture millions of automobiles, trucks, highways and local road systems required for their use, became the hallmarks of our nation's portrait shortly after the inception of the twentieth century.

However, as this frenetic activity of production and construction continued there emerged, in what has been euphemistically labeled the "gilded age," i.e. the period between 1875-1900 this era of industrial capitalism began to reflect enormous inequality between those plutocrats who had founded these empires and so many Americans whose lives were barely self-sustaining.

Beyond the chasms of income and asset accumulation separated this miniscule group of millionaires from their American compatriots, was an evolving normative perspective which suggested those who succeeded in their efforts to amass wealth were deserving of this success, and those whose economic realities were grim were responsible for their plight, as well. Thus, those efforts to institute and sustain fiscal policies and programs sought to mitigate their impoverishment and slightly reduce the affluence of those who were so fortunate, were fiercely resisted. In fact, these conflicts about those issues relative to inequality, economic and educational opportunity, and the redistributionist impulses incorporated into progressive taxation schedules subsequent to the establishment of the national income tax in 1913, have periodically resurfaced.

These disagreements would continue to be sources of friction, rhetorical combat, and physical violence throughout the twentieth century, as well as during our current era when these inequities are assuming unique capacities to inflict ever-greater damage upon so many of our citizens, whose view of the lives their children will inherit is extremely pessimistic.

When the Great Depression occurred in autumn of 1929, and 25% of our citizens became unemployed not long thereafter, those who comprised the industrialist class were persuaded by President Roosevelt in order to salvage the capitalist economy of this nation they would be compelled to increase the magnitude of taxes they provided to the federal government. These funds were allocated to support a host of public employment projects to expand and repair our nation's infrastructure, provide opportunities to the unemployed to acquire skills through the vehicles of job training programs, and support a public arts program to employ artists photographers, filmmakers, and dramatists. Thus, by acquiescing to F.D.R.'s demands and significantly increasing their fiscal obligations this class of plutocrats assumed, they were reluctant contributors to their financial salvation.

However, with our involvement in the Second World War as the result of the Japanese attack on Pearl Harbor, our economy roared back to life, and because we were exempt from the destruction and massive loss of life which occurred in Europe, the Soviet Union, and the "Far East," as the hostilities concluded, we emerged as the world's preeminent economic colussus.

The decades thereafter were enormously productive with little international competition American industry exploded during the 1950's and 1960's as we simultaneously struggled to contain the virulence and expansion of Communism in much of the developing world, in a posture of primary competition with the Soviet Union, and the People's Republic of China.

As the South Vietnam conflict became a full-fledged war involving hundreds of thousands of our military, this struggle in concert with long-simmering domestic concerns regarding racism, and the denial of civil liberties for many African Americans became a fully rendered political conflagration, which roiled our nation throughout the balance of this decade.

In addition, a movement, principally among university students and other elements of the American intellectual and politically influential segments, arose to pose seminal questions and assert the country's social and economic institutions and values were in grievous need of revamping. The alternative cultural reality they championed would provide greater equality, educational opportunity, self-actualization, and sexual freedom than the arrangements existing at that moment in our historic journey. Moreover, the nation had "rediscovered" the existence of poverty in many urban and rural sections of our democracy that was both widespread and stubbornly intractable. Estimates of the magnitude of the underprivileged class hovered between 15% and 20% of our population.

All these cultural cross-currents regarding various aspects of our foreign policy, domestic structures, and the quality of life within hierarchical institutions, in both the private sector and public bureaucracies, had fostered an alienation from these sources of conformity and regimentation. In the view of many, especially among our youth, these systems were mind-deadening, morally bankrupt, bereft of joy and creative passion, and precluded the possible expression of any meaningful form of freedom and individual fulfillment.

The decade of the 1960's, in retrospect, produced significant alterations in the social and behavioral landscape of the U.S. Emasculating Puritan sexual mores were relaxed and the colonialism, which our involvement in Vietnam represented, was ultimately repudiated as the result of massive and continuing protests and marches throughout this country.

The denial of both voting rights and the persistent patterns of segregation (particularly in the South) imposed upon African Americans were repealed and discarded as the derivative of substantial citizen demands, the actions of the federal government, and the Supreme Court. In addition, the stultifying conformity and repression of individualistic expression by those who labored in major bureaucracies, be they private or public in character, were called into question and these pernicious influences upon the persona, spirit, and the creative humanity of those in their employ, were substantially mitigated. These agents of change sought an enhanced capacity for democratic participation within the workplace and beyond, within the perimeters of decision-making that occurred in the larger macro political framework at the municipal, county, regional, state, or federal level. Thus, in some intrinsic regard, the very central value system, as well as the bedrock institutions of this country, was challenged in a frontal assault. As a result, much was achieved by these forces in many areas of our culture. The principal accomplishments reduced racism, enlarged the sphere of involvement within formal and informal mechanisms and processes in the private sector and public sphere by which decisions were reached, and allowed for greater self-expression in terms of our personal muse and with regard to our sexual liberation.

However, as the 1970's dawned, regressive forces attempted to rescind what had been accomplished during the previous decade. Their campaigns to expand their commercial enterprises beyond the shores of the U.S. as well as the cultural arrangements and economic institutions they fiercely advocated, lacked legitimacy in the view of many citizens. To invalidate and discredit these perceptions, a sustained and multilevel rebuttal by the forces of the status quo was implemented. As a result, this coterie of wealthy industrialists mounted a comprehensive, multitier campaign to reassert an unquestioned hegemony and national allegiance to the ascendant structure of values that had been so severely damaged by the liberating activism of the decade that had just concluded.

Substantial sums were allocated to fund institutes and centers, which incessantly trumpeted the message of the ideological perspectives which the enormously affluent embraced, and which, if socially reinvigorated, augured the continued dominance of those institutional structures that were extant. Moreover, this decade replaced a central concern of the previous period, i.e. a conscious dedication and commitment to the welfare of those who had historically been excluded from freedoms and opportunities in this nation, and the consequences of that exclusion, such as poverty and oppression.

What became an overriding priority instead was the concept of the "me decade;" a premeditated campaign to remove the nation's focus from the ills and discrimination of our cultural topography and the requisite actions required to ameliorate these injustices to a consideration of personal material achievement and social hedonism.

Throughout this decade the self-indulgent mantras of the exploration of our personal interior consciousness, the unceasing analysis of our physical being, and our individual and entirely subjective preferences and desires dominated our cultural consciousness. These forms of self-inquiry and analysis were broadly encouraged, and this process of navel contemplation displaced virtually all vestiges of a larger empathy for those whose lives remained bleak and economically fragile. Thus, pluralism, altruism, empathy, and compassion were preempted by the national pursuit of personal indulgence and unrelenting self-absorption.

In addition to this myopic and insular quest for solipsistic self-expression, this decade was the time period in which some in our academic settings formulated and enunciated the normative content of a philosophy of neo-conservative perspectives.

Milton Freidman at Chicago and Arthur Laffer at USC, among others, asserted the source of our cultural ills was a huge sprawling federal government that became impossible to effectively manage. Moreover, the concomitant expenditures of federal revenues were responsible for eroding individual initiative in our society, and for the creation and maintenance of a permanent class of citizens whose very viability was dependent on continual federal largesse.

In addition, they contended the most prospectively efficient mode of economic growth would be derived from the notion "a rising tide lifts all boats," i.e. with the appropriate incentives, such as a diminished capital gains tax rate, the extraordinarily wealthy would infuse substantial investments into the expansion of industrial capacity, research, and development. Moreover, they argued these policies would spur technological advances that would produce greater productivity and, as a result, these actions would enlarge our GNP and create a significant increase in those who were employed at wages levels that would sustain and augment those who were securely ensconced in the nation's middle-class.

This worldview remained in the ascendancy in the executive suites of America's industrial and post-industrial elites, and was the primary value system that animated the federal government's activities, policies, and program initiatives, under the hegemony of Ronald Reagan, and continued its dominance throughout the advent of the new millennium. However, those who were responsible for the transformation of our economy during this thirty year period, from a society engaged in the production of goods and the provision of services, to a culture in which arcane financial transactions represented a major portion of the profits, which financial services sector of our economy had produced, collapsed in 2008. This implosion occurred under the weight of the cupidity and reckless and immoral pursuit by Wall Street of unconscionable levels of profitability, and the compensation packages they formulated, for themselves and their compatriots, throughout other major global financial centers.

As the 1970's yielded to the Reagan era, the "me decade" succumbed to an unprecedented "critical mass" of stock brokers and financial specialists, who were animated by aspirations of material wealth and career trajectories to the corporate pinnacle, with all the influence and power, which flowed from those realities, and thus, was the "Yuppie" generation created. Moreover, this period witnessed the advent of "globalization" with initially a trickle of Fortune 500 companies deserting their domestic manufacturing facilities in order to establish these production capabilities in China, India, and other countries where labor costs were but a fraction of the wage scales a unionized American work force had secured. These hard won compensation packages, which laborers had secured, were the result of decades of collective bargaining tactics, strikes, boycotts, and Congressional support as well as favorable legal decisions at the state and federal levels of adjudication. In other developing nations where poverty was rampant, employment opportunities were scant and miserably compensated, and where government was, ineffectual or virtually non-existent this impotency deprived their citizens of the capability to protect critical environmental resources as they contractually engaged with transnational behemoths.

During the final years of the twentieth century, the momentum of corporations relocating their manufacturing capacities to foreign countries accelerated, and in the wake of their departure urban centers, towns, and rural areas that had, for decades, played host to these commercial enterprises began to unravel. These entities had derived vital governmental income from tax schedules to provide public services. Moreover, the general economic well-being, which these jobs represented, was initially significantly reduced and ultimately, when these facilities ceased production altogether, these sources of income completely evaporated.

This exodus left behind a trail of empty buildings, former employees who received unemployment insurance, and when these benefits were exhausted, welfare payments, and local governments were compelled to slash services and due to bond and other financial obligations assumed in a rosier economic era, become supplicants at the state trough.

The specter of default loomed largely on these obligations and so too did litigation and legislative punishments for their "fiscal imprudence." As a result, numerous local governments had no alternative but to seek whatever protections which a bankruptcy status might confer.

Concurrent with this activity, the focus of the nation's financial community began to enlarge its scope beyond the traditional investment areas, such as the expansion of corporate production and services, loans to consumers for automobiles and finance college educations, as well as the construction of office buildings, malls, and the nation's hospitality and travel segments. Beyond the previous realms of activity, an evolving interest in creating and sustaining those transactions that relied on the fluctuations of the global financial marketplace vis a vis sovereign currencies, and other financial mechanisms and processes, to produce vast profits and augment the balance sheets and net worth of these banking institutions, seize their imaginations. Distinctions between the permissible activities of various commercial banks and activities in which investment banks, newly emerging hedge funds, and venture capitalists, were engaged were dismantled; as well as a reduction in reserve capital requirements necessary to ensure stability and solvency, should a portion of their loan portfolios be adversely affected.

The stock markets began a dramatic ascendency during this period that endured for a quarter of a century. The real estate market also commenced a dizzying climb as the assigned values to these homes skyrocketed to levels unprecedented and astronomical. Investment funds truly global in their appetites created ever more coordination between central banks and major private financial institutions throughout the industrial nations, and increasingly developing countries as the result of the increased presence of American and European manufacturing elements, allocated their resources to these transactions. An additional source of capital was derived from the exploding volume of international trade of commodities, agricultural produce, and natural resources. As a result, these "emerging economies" became investors in the sophisticated and exponentially expanding universe of credit default swaps, reinsurance programs, and numerous forms of arbitrage.

But, perhaps the most critical distinction that characterized this period of investment activity, as the result of the internationalization of investment portfolios marketed to institutional investors around the globe was the previous crucial personal relationships that had been reflected with regard to the financing of real estate acquisitions, was abrogated. When these purchases represented the principal residence of the families involved, in the previous era individual banks that issued these loans were usually situated in the community. More importantly, these entities had established and sustained the trust of their banking customers by reflecting ethical patterns of behavior and competence in the management of their investments, and consumer loan practices from the inception of their existence as lending institutions.

That crucial link between lender and loan recipient dissolved as we entered the twenty-first century, and through such instruments as credit default swaps, and other esoteric quantitative models and techniques these loans, that comprised massive offerings to institutional investors from many nations, grew exponentially. What compounded this travesty was the fact neither the creditworthiness of the buyer nor the responsibility of the entity providing these funds; in the event of a default attributable to declining market circumstances became incapable of meeting their financial obligations, were contractual prerequisites.

What these banks and investment funds were concerned with was the profit reaped by the sale of these portfolios, and the compensation levels and bonuses their efforts, if successful in these transactions, would generate for the individual broker and the firm in which he labored.

As the first decade of the twenty-first century progressed, increasing risk was assumed through the pervasive involvement of an influx within the financial services sector of a stream of graduates from prestigious MBA programs, who came to Wall Street armed with sophisticated models of economic analysis and prognostication. These "Quants" (i.e. those who had in their academic studies pursued primarily quantitative methods of assessment and formulations, upon which their predictions and forecasts of human behavior were predicated), were prophets of unmitigated profitability.

In such complex transactions as arbitrage, capitalizing on the minute fluctuations of various sovereign currencies in their daily trading interrelationships with each other, and in other credit derivative instruments that would ensure, regardless of the markets direction, the financial risks of these institutions would be indemnified by insurance companies and others who had assumed positions of exposure, and as a result the solvency of these institutions would be uncompromised.

These spurious and delusional presumptions collided with the brutal reality of the unraveling of Lehman brothers in the autumn of 2008, and the prospect if extraordinary measures were not immediately invoked by the federal government, a depression of such protracted length and severity would be the immediate future in which our nation would be engulfed, would dwarf in magnitude and virulence, the suffering, which so many of our citizens experienced subsequent to the crash of 1929, became a shattering reality.

It was in order to avert the bankruptcy of such automotive giants as General Motors, and Chrysler, and the imminent self-destruction of such financial institutions as Countrywide Financial, and Citi Bank, and the insurance behemoth AIG, throughout the period that extended until 2013, trillions of dollars were provided by the Federal Reserve at virtually non-existent interest rates, to ensure these institutions, which were deemed "too big to fail," remained viable.

A mere fraction of these sums were provided by Congressional fiat to the millions of Americans whose jobs were abolished by a ferociously contracting economy and who, in many instances, were incapable of meeting their mortgage obligations, and thus became homeless as major banks throughout every section of our nation set into motion the juggernaut of wholesale and often indiscriminate foreclosure proceedings..

The value of residential real estate plummeted to levels that had not been in evidence in some instances in this nation for forty years. Major banks, though the recipient of trillions of dollars from the treasury, imposed new and in some instances draconian requirements upon those who had previously been responsible for the loans they incurred, for which few individuals or smaller companies could now qualify, and thus were rejected, and as a result our national economic deterioration expanded and accelerated. Had the dollar not been the world's official reserve currency it is doubtful through the process of purchasing U.S. bonds by sovereign governments principally the PRC, Japan, South Korea, and our treasury's issuance of trillions of dollars during this period, the nation could have retained its status as both a viable economy and the world's dominant economic system.

However, these activities were responsible for greatly exacerbating, in both quantitative and qualitative terms, the magnitude of our indebtedness in both the realms of deficits and the costs of servicing our debt, i.e. interest payments as well as the continuing imbalances reflected in our trading relationships, to our financial detriment. For those who argue vehemently technology's continuing advances and innovation will be the salvation of our current disastrous financial reality, I would remind them the cell phone and the Internet, with all the implications of their explosive proliferation throughout the globe in terms of the revenues generated by such companies as Nokia, Motorola, Apple, and Samsung, had not produced that result. Moreover, the continuing extensive enlargement in the developing world through crucial advances relative to communications mobility and access to virtually unlimited repositories of information, the impact they are currently registering is quantitative in its implications and no longer a qualitative revolution, if it ever was. These technologies were introduced more than two decades ago and have not altered, in any meaningful regard, the fundamental realities of the global distribution of wealth or the significant diminution of poverty.

In the United States, these systems of communication and information have achieved greater efficiency and productivity in the operations of many transnational companies. However, the preponderant portion of these gains found their way into the compensation of senior executives, rather than the average employee. What these technologies have also accomplished, via the ubiquitous national network of cell towers and email, is to render virtually meaningless the distinction of workplace from our residencies.

Many people find themselves, compulsively, going online to their various accounts to ensure they have remained abreast of any and all developments, internal to their company's activities and the universe of personal relationships and the world of domestic and foreign developments occurring.

But, perhaps most ominously, such federal agencies as the NSA, the CIA and Homeland Security have created and sustained the massive collection of data, personal phone records, email transcripts, as well as aspects of our financial and medical histories, that expand into the realm of the compromise of our constitutional rights of privacy, in the name of protecting our nation from the intentions of global terrorists.

At this moment in time, there does not exist technologies that contain the potential to transform our economic system regarding meaningful employment opportunities for the unemployed or those such as the legitimately aggrieved residents of Ferguson, Missouri who have as many African-Americans throughout this nation, been consigned to urban and rural enclaves of neglect, indifference, and unremitting poverty.

Finally, as we complete our review of the most salient variables and dynamics of the evolution of the American capitalist system, our focus demands an exploration of the current topography and principal activity operative in the realm of our economy and our political system.

The central circumstances of 2015 are the facts of a U.S. with unprecedented unemployment levels since the Great Depression. The reality of those who appear on the Forbes 400 list of the wealthiest Americans possess an aggregate wealth that exceeds the asset value of 180 million Americans that comprise the middleclass and poor, as corporate profits soar and the financial status of the middleclass continues its erosion. In addition the "working poor" continue to receive a minimum wage totally inadequate to support themselves, as millions of African American men throughout the country reside in towns and cities in which police forces (principally Caucasian) treat these citizens as an occupying army might regard its enemies, frequently engaging in abuse, brutality, and the disregard of the civil rights of these individuals. The growth of what was a trickle into a surging river of companies who are engaging in the corporate tactic of "inversion," i.e.

American companies deserting the U.S. in terms of the physical location of their corporate headquarters as the result of mergers with foreign corporations, and establishing these entities in other countries in which their tax liabilities are more modest. A congress that continues in a posture of ferocious partisanship in the unrelenting grip of inactivity and dysfunction, as pressing national priorities such as immigration reform, the revamping of our tax codes for both individuals and companies, the continuing disintegration of our infrastructure with all neglect signifies for our economy regarding a lack of middleclass jobs and our general competitiveness in a world of ever-intensifying competition. In addition, our public education systems at the K-12 levels, despite some exceptions in the arena of charter schools and experimental approaches to transforming the entire social environment in which these students live, remains mired in mediocrity. Moreover, these institutions are incapable of equipping those who come from broken homes, suffer from inadequate nutrition, and reside in unsafe neighborhoods with the skills and information to become literate and perform basic mathematical calculations required to formulate family budgets or master textbooks manuals and other instruction materials, that require a reading facility beyond those capacities frequently developed in a primary grade school setting.

With regard to those rare decisions forthcoming from Congress, their general tone and tenor is to protect the advantages and privileges of the nation's one percent, and rarely, if ever particularly in regard to the Republican House Majority, issue legislative initiatives that reduce the tax burdens of the middleclass or provide accessible pathways to this relatively comfortable status, from the ranks of those who dwell in poverty.

To ensure the rancor and divisiveness between the conservative and more liberal elements of our population continue and are exacerbated, various PAC's and other nonprofit organizations have greatly increased their donations to the Tea Party, and to those who oppose gay marriage and support the relaxation of regulatory prohibitions regarding the pollution emissions of major energy conglomerates. In addition, these groups donate to extremists who remain steadfast in their opposition to increasing the minimum wage, and championing for those approximately twelve million Hispanics a pathway to citizenship that is impossible in its requirements and interminable as to the chronology in which it might be accomplished.

The overwhelming majority of Congressional districts, as the result of unceasing Gerrymandering by local courts, are not competitive. Those who have successfully attained their seats in Congress are rarely dislodged.

Incumbency confers an enormous advantage from a financial standpoint and an electoral perspective. All that is required of these public servants is they do not incite or alienate their constituencies as the result of votes in their respective chambers or public statements regarding controversial policies or embattled government programs, with which significant numbers of their district residents are in fervent disagreement.

Since the Great Recession, the numbers of entrepreneurs who are founding companies has significantly declined as the result of a diminution in the ranks of those who are expanding the frontiers of research and development in general, and in regard to specific technologies in particular that reflect the potential to generate meaningful sales of these products in either the hardware/software arenas. Moreover, the general economic climate is vastly more competitive among those in the U.S. who are seeking employment opportunities, as the trends instituted in the past two decades, i.e. the delegation to contractors and sub-contractors, of the management of many franchise locations has enabled such companies as McDonald's to intensify these predispositions.

The incentives to undertake these contractual relationships is to relieve themselves of such traditional financial obligations as healthcare, paid vacation periods, sick leave, and, most importantly, afford the capability to craft work schedules that are longer and frequently bereft of overtime levels of compensation.

Corporate representatives, when inquiries are posed, claim these practices are attributable not to their company's policies or wishes, but rather to the practices and actions of the firms which McDonald's has retained to operate and administer these facilities, i.e. franchisees.

Americans are devoting greater periods of time to commuting between their places of employment and their homes as roadways and highways become ever more congested, and the required repairs/expansion of these elements of our national infrastructure are ignored and neglected. As these bridges, tunnels, harbors, and through-fares age and the maintenance schedules necessary to sustain their structural viability are disregarded, increasing numbers of these crucial transportations components are closed due to lack of safety, or actually fail during use with the resulting tragic loss of life and the litigation/settlement costs which the families of survivors often receive, greatly eclipses those funds required to properly maintain these structures.

For those who are currently employed, longer hours in their factories, offices, and in the transportation of goods and the provision of services are often required. As a result of these professional obligations, the stress, anxiety, and the inherent insecurity of these positions, become onerous. Moreover, because of the enormous number of unemployed that are desperate for any wage producing involvement, should an employee balk at the terms and conditions of his involvement with an organization, the numbers of unemployed who are clamoring for that position are astronomical.

In addition, because of the dramatic decline of unionized workplaces which in previous decades were capable of protecting workers from unjust or arbitrary disciplinary action and or termination, the current environment is infinitely more precarious.

Fifty years ago, more than one third of the private sector corporations were unionized; today that statistic has been diminished to approximately seven percent, and in the public sector but one-third of the current employee complement are union members. To cope with the additional stress and fatigue, anxiety, and uncertainties, which these elongated work schedules imposed during this period, the American public ingested approximately $300 billion of anti-depressant medications, sleeping pills, and anti-anxiety compounds in 2014. Others seek the blissful refuge of alcohol to deaden their apprehensions and anesthetize their insecurities, or the adulterated and care-free oblivion of such non-prescription drugs as marijuana, heroin, or cocaine, frequently becoming as the result of recurring use of these substances addicts, and all that flows from that imprisonment in terms of horrendous marital, financial, career, law-enforcement, judicial, and interpersonal ramifications.

As the erosion of middleclass financial circumstance continues to unravel, the pressures to maintain the viability of the family's material circumstances increase greatly. Often, both adults in a household are compelled to assume additional employment responsibilities to generate the income to meet their expenses.

The physical and mental demands of these multiple involvements further drain the energies and abilities of those who are parents, and the quality of the domestic environment is degraded by conflict and exhaustion, and as a result, the children in these situations often experience a sense of neglect and indifference, and the evolution of the resentments and rancor and unhappiness which these reactions provoke.

Frequently, as they become adolescents they will seek from peers and others who represent authority figures in their lives, the consolation and caring which has been greatly diminished or is now totally absent in their family dynamics. These conditions often breed the development of unsavory or pathological relationships that rob these young adults of their innocence, introduce them to lives of criminal behavior, and should arrest records be created to reflect their anti-social activities, the consequences of these involvements can cause enormously difficulty for these individuals in expunging their juvenile histories and creating an adult life of purpose, integrity, and achievement. Moreover, these significant and profound lapses of ethical misjudgment and grievous error can deprive those who may harbor the desire to serve their country in a branch of the American military this opportunity as we, in the era of a post-Iraq and our imminent departure from Afghanistan, will result in a total force that will be significantly reduced.

Given the substantial numbers of young men and women whose employment prospects are grim because they are armed only with high-school diplomas, and who have not engaged in illegal activities, those chosen to serve will be drawn almost exclusively from this cohort of law-abiding young adults.

Beyond the portrait of a nation in which these pathologies are prominent features of our social and cultural topography, we continue our decline vis-a-vis other industrial nations in virtually every category of comparison, i.e. health indicators, "happiness" measurements, social cohesion, inter-class enmity, educational accomplishments, personal alienation and fragmentation parameters. These qualitative and quantitative assessments cumulatively derive from the fundamental awareness of increasing numbers of Americans, our current malaise and pessimism are in the final analysis a betrayal of those commitments and obligations our Founding Fathers and successive generations of reformers who have labored so mightily to extend to all our citizens. Moreover, it is also a continuing act of infidelity to the processes and procedures they reflect to translate the noble concepts upon which our country was established, into a dynamic and organic national sovereignty.

In numerous discussions I have held with colleagues and associates about these matters, there usually emerges a substantial consensus that supports the validity of the previously enunciated evaluation of our cotemporary social circumstances. Moreover, frequently a companionate sentiment emerges as well, that the prospects and possibilities of rectifying these injustices, and in some truly meaningful regard is not possible. Altering our cultural trajectory to achieve an infinitely more just and exuberant and joyous future for our citizens, is beyond our capacities as individuals and a society to accomplish, and thus do the twin scourges of defeat and impotence announce their arrival.

To those who espouse these defeatist sentiments and suggest whatever efforts are mounted and activities initiated will produce little if anything toward the mitigation of these malignant ills, I say that to embrace that perspective is to ensure the continuation of the present trends and to guarantee an American future of intensifying crisis and dissolution that will ultimately be a witness to the conclusion of our audacious experiment in representative democracy. Though the challenges we confront our enormously difficult to surmount and will require the concerted efforts of millions of Americans to accomplish, in a struggle against institutions who have at their command huge resources and a history of succeeding in their attempts to ensure, however discontent, sullen, or unhappy the majority of our population may become, they remain divided, overwhelmed, and deprived of those capacities necessary to accomplish the goal of a rejuvenated homeland.

The campaign to rescue our country from those who wish its continued subjugation will be lengthy and arduous; however, we have demonstrated throughout our history a united populace is capable of extraordinary achievements.

To intentionally recast Edmund Burke's dictum, "All that is required for democracy to fail is the continued inactivity of good men," it is my contention what is necessary for the creation and maintenance of a just society is for men and women, in the service of its attainment, to remain unfailing and ferocious in their exertions.

Thus, this introduction concludes. It is my hope the preceding analysis has been a valuable introduction to the reader to more fully comprehend the nature and content of the forces, influences, and institutions in our society responsible for our deplorable current miasma. However, in order to embark upon a cultural campaign that will produce the maximal redress of our economic and political grievances, it is critical for us to become completely conversant with the tools and tactics, which these plutocrats deploy unceasingly, to prevent and substantially frustrate the aspirations of those among us who wish an infinitely more democratic America.

I will provide a comprehensive insight into this "playbook of the plutocrats" in Chapter One. For once, we have become familiar with the instrumentalities and strategies that undergird them, will it be possible to mount a multi-tier agenda of action to diminish and ultimately incapacitate these forces, and restore this nation to its proper and rightful course of conduct and in pursuit of a destination we embarked upon more than two centuries ago.

CHAPTER ONE

The Techniques and Technologies
of Ensuring a Compliant American Nation

T hose at the apogee of our society are enormously sophisticated regarding the modalities they employ to ensure the relative calm and acquiescence of our citizens. This multi-tier approach ensures a critical mass of repudiation of our ascendant ideology and the institutional arrangements, which render this value system operational, does not coalesce. This strategy contains elements of governmental subservience (at all levels) the total spectrum of mass media that support and reiterate these principles and normative notions, and the unceasing vocalization of patriotic celebrations of historical mythology and contemporary observances.

At the epicenter of this recipe to ensure our fervent national allegiance to these concepts, is the notion of our "exceptional" and exalted status among all nations that comprise the global community. In addition, are we assailed by the constant bombardment of our senses and consciousness with hollow trivia and fraudulent conflicts and personal enmities on the Internet, and integral to the ever-expanding prurient content of cable television offerings, which seek to enlarge the images of blatant sexual behavior and character presentations, which become ever more debased and pathological.

The creation of PAC's and other non-profit entities that provide contributions to organizations designed to exploit and intensify those fissures and disagreements among our electorate with regard to such issues as immigration reform, gay marriage, racial and religious schisms and animosities, and, most importantly, the National Tea Party movement, which has become so adroit at terrorizing moderates in both parties, and whose ultimate goal is to bring this government to its knees in a posture of total dysfunction and virulent partisan debate. Since 2010, with its unveiling and current position of political prominence, it has been quite successful in accomplishing a state of dysfunction, rancor, and personal enmities among those in Congress with the result that almost nothing of substantive legislative consequence to resolve these disputes has been enacted into law. However, it is within these hallowed halls of responsiveness to the wishes of our economic royalty, and in other components of the federal government, their agendas and priorities have been realized.

During the period reflected in the Reagan hegemony and in the years beyond that, including the George W. Bush presidency, the following major capacities regarding multi-national activity has been legitimized:

- In 1982, the SEC rescinded the rule which forbade corporations from repurchasing unlimited numbers of their shares of stock on the open market.[1]

- Encouraged by the Reagan administration's assault on the Air Traffic Controllers' Union, many major corporations began their own efforts to diminish the power of unions that represented the interest of their workers, and ultimately to seek their total emasculation. Ibid

- The historical pattern which persisted from the period of the Second World War until the 1980's, reflected the retention of their earnings and their reinvestment in business expansion, new or improved technologies, employee training programs, and wage increases for their workers. Ibid

- In the period between 2003 and 2012, more than 449 companies listed on the Fortune 500 devoted 54% of their net earnings to the repurchase of their equity shares and 37% of these proceeds for dividends to shareholders. Thus, a paltry 9% of these profits were allocated to investments, research and development, expansion of manufacturing, operational or administrative capacities, cash reserves, and virtually nothing for wage increases to their employees. Iibid

- The ten companies devoted $859 billion to the repurchase of their shares provided their CEO's with 58% of their compensation in stock shares or options. Ibid

- Cisco Systems devoted 121% of its profits to stock repurchases, dividends, and executive pay; stock shares or options to their CEO – The 21% reflects the company's action to issue corporate bonds, and thus, assume debt to absorb the actual expenses of their company's operations. Ibid

- Amidst all this profitability, soaring stock prices, dividend streams, and astronomical compensation to CEO's, U.S. companies are incurring unprecedented levels of indebtedness in order to enrich their shareholders and themselves and their executive colleagues. Ibid

- Moreover, though the tax on U.S. corporations currently approaches 35%, through their army of lobbyists and lawyers and the numerous tax loopholes created and exploited by these experts, the average tax payment by these companies to discharge their annual IRS obligations was but 13%.

In the final analysis, the principal conclusion the author of the essay "Profits Without Prosperity" in the September 2014 issue of Harvard Business Review, William Lazonick, a professor of economics at the University of Massachusetts at Lowell, is the rate of return on investment exceeds the rate of economic growth. As a result, wealth in this nation is derived principally from *retarding businesses' abilities to invest in growth engendering activity.* The fundamental raison d'etre of modern U.S. corporations is to reward investors and senior executives with income previously allocated to expansion, research and development, training, and to increase the wages of their employees.

This stark and extraordinarily unnerving reality about the contemporary actions of these companies is, if left uncorrected, our system of capitalism will remain a nation that welcomes and enriches investors, while those that comprise the ranks of working Americans will be provided with little but a stream of income that does nothing but barely sustain the viability of themselves and their families.

The current economic circumstances invert the historic purpose of commercial enterprises founded and prospered during the nineteenth and twentieth centuries. Their establishment was to provide various products and services that would enable citizens to reduce the tedium and toil that cluttered their domestic and professional calendars. If these firms were competent and reflected integrity in their business operations and relations with the public, and the wares they sold were affordable and of enduring quality, these companies would generate substantial revenues and profitability as the result of the esteem in which they were held by our nation's consumers. A derivative of that reality was those who invested in and were responsible for the operations and success of these entities were handsomely compensated, and their employees, by virtue of their efforts and productive capabilities, were also recipients of wages and salaries that provided them access to a comfortable middleclass existence.

In our current period of economic activity, the principal objective is to enhance the wealth of investors, unceasingly elevate the value of the corporation's equity, and provide seven, eight, and, in some instances, nine figures compensation packages to the most senior executives while the manufacture and sale of products and provision of services are relegated to a secondary, if not tertiary, role of importance. Moreover, their employees' wages and benefits packages continue to stagnate and, in some instances, have declined since the Great Recession of 2008, the numbers of currently vacant jobs stands at approximately four million, while the ranks of the unemployed and under-employed exceeds twenty-three million individuals.

As relevant as these statistics are to defining the central component of our current lamentable national circumstance, they reflect but a portion of the total social and cultural capability that ensures the docility and inactivity of so many of our citizens. The spectrum of tools and tactics deployed in the service of the maintenance of our social arrangements eclipses any attempts of the ruling classes in the historical record of previous civilizations to sustain and enlarge their influence and dominion. The contemporary modalities deployed reflect an infinitely more subtle and extensive political, social, and psychological forces that utilize the media, many university based institutions, the reiteration of patriotic ideologies and ceremonies which bear ever less relevance to our contemporary cultural realities, and the incessant bombardment of our senses by advertising messages to stoke the fires of envy and material acquisitiveness. In addition, we are assailed by the constant assault on our senses and consciousness with hollow trivia and fraudulent conflicts and personal enmities on the Internet, and integral to the ever-expanding prurient content of cable television offerings which seek to enlarge the images of blatant sexual behavior and character presentations, which become ever more debased and pathological.

Reality shows that depict aspects of the human personality that are mean-spirited, hyper-competitive, and intentionally scripted to foment conflict and contentiousness within the families involved about matters with little substance and less meaning, continue to proliferate. The imprisonment of many by the Internet, which is consulted incessantly throughout the day and evening lest our knowledge of the gossip, intrigue, and scandals that surround "celebrities" grow stale and dated.

The tidal wave of spam and the commercial opportunities contained within that universe, generated twenty-four hours each day for our review and investigation, further beckons us to acquire more of what has scant value, and dwell on the messages that reinvigorate our insecurities and comparative failings when measured against the skills and accomplishments of others who are equipped with various talents, physical properties, or superficial attainments.

The Multi-tiered Choreography
Which Enables Titans of Finance to Retain Their Dominion

Perhaps the analogy that most accurately describes the process and procedures by which are society is "managed" is the a multi-disciplinary composition of the total gamut of skills and expertise, which is frequently summoned to meetings to address various political and economic and military crises in the Situation Room of the White House.

Though the individuals who comprise this group function are less formally constituted, and often serve in "ad hoc" capacities, principally from the senior most echelons of the private sector, they encompass among their ranks a broad range of expertise in such disciplines as political strategic analysis, economic systems and policies, psychological assessments and evaluations, public opinion, polling skills, and social issues exploration. In attendance, pundits conversant with media trends and entertainment preferences, advertising and public relations techniques and campaigns, as well as a sprinkling of intelligence and law-enforcement officials, and perhaps, most importantly, representatives who sit at the tables of international banking and global economic development bodies, such as the World Bank, the IMF, and various UN commissions and committees. Though the preceding enumeration may not be exhaustive, it most certainly manifests the principal components of those areas of greatest interest and concern to the community of American plutocrats.

For those of you who are dismissing my assertions as simply another rant of the lunatic fringe regarding the matter of "conspiratorial powers" that rule surreptitiously and subliminally in this nation, you risk, by this interpretation, a total misconstruing of what I am suggesting. Those who comprise this nation's elite frequently interact with one another in various settings, conferences, seminars at Davos, Aspen, Washington, and social networks in which they spend leisurely summer afternoons at elegant country clubs playing golf and tennis matches, and feasting sumptuously. These CEO's and others at the apogee of the multinational corporations are in the unceasing receipt of dispatches, communiques, press releases, etc. prepared and disseminated by their phalanx of lobbyists, consultants, lawyers, and public relations staffs. These individuals devote their entire consciousness to monitoring evaluating and analyzing virtually all developments of a social, political, and economic character that might significantly impact the welfare and future prospects of these companies.

In the event these unfolding events serve their interests, they will actively support them. In those instances which presage poorly for their economic and strategic aspirations, they will devise various tactics involving elements of their constituencies to ensure these regulators, policies, and legislative initiatives are soundly defeated. The agendas and objectives of this broad swath of corporate America though occasionally engaged in minor conflicts and disagreements, are usually united in their fundamental goals, i.e. the maintenance of the status quo with regard to their current patterns of "investment capitalism," and the enlargement of their international footprints and the streams of revenue and profitability, that flow from that process of expansion.

Beyond those normative perspectives, which are embraced unanimously by our moguls, are the primary organizing principles which they create and ferociously deploy to ensure the compliance of virtually all other citizens who are subordinate, and those are the instruments of entrenched apprehension, rampant anxiety, intensifying insecurities, and escalating stress. How more effectively than the multiple facets of fear can potentially sullen, discontented, and resistant elements, of our nation be managed? Particularly, as it relates to our macro-economic circumstances, and thus, with regard to our individual financial prospects, our lives coerced and restricted to little more than which retains the physical integrity of our households and our families. Thus, we witness at the current moment approximately six candidates for every job vacancy. Wage scales, which remain virtually frozen for most employees, preclude advances to a more secure foothold in the middleclass.

For those millions of Americans who are mired in poverty, i.e. the poor who remain barely viable as the result of federal and, in some instances, the entirely inadequate subsistence of state funds, and their lives are becoming ever more grim and demoralizing. Their existences consist of inadequate nutrition, bouts of hunger when monthly food stamp allotments are exhausted, and a consciousness that dreads the ever-present specter of freezing winters in structurally unsound rooms and apartments, and broiling summers in these quarters. They suffer from continuing vulnerability to the criminal depredations of neighbors, as well as access to schools, which do very little to prepare their children for lives in which literacy and mathematics are essential to navigate complex and demanding interpersonal and employment transactions. In addition, they are frequently afflicted with the premature onset of hypertension, heart disease, cancer, obesity, diabetes, and other ailments destroying their health and greatly abbreviating their lifespans. There exists in these disintegrating neighborhoods the ever-present temptation of drugs and alcohol to deaden their suffering and anesthetize the unremitting terrors, which a life under these physical, economic, and social circumstances produces, in tragically abundant measure. The millions who dwell in these conditions can be found in many urban cores and rural enclaves. Also are those who have been abandoned by many major American companies in their unceasing search to establish business enterprises in countries where wage scales are a fraction of those required by U.S. workers to maintain a middle-class existence, and where environmental restrictions are lax or non-existent.

It is in these geographical settings where despots susceptible to lucrative inducements who ensure the terms and conditions of these economic agreements and arrangements, permit these corporations to extract enormous resources, and thus, generate huge profits. What ensures the relative calm and acquiescence of these populations is not contentment or satisfaction with the quality of their lives, but the menacing and militarized presence of law enforcement agencies usually composed of disproportionate numbers of Caucasian males who are charged with responsibility of policing significant numbers of minority residents, primarily African American and Hispanic.

These occupying armies, through their brutal tactics and indifference to civil liberties, continually remind those who dwell in these cities and towns that any behavior that challenges the status quo will be harshly suppressed. Even those activities constitutionally permitted regarding protests and marches and other political forms of resistance to the abysmal quality of life in which they are mired, as well as any behavior that seeks in any mode that is non-violent to alter and improve their material circumstances, will be met with fierce and lethal responses.

The judicial system in these regions and a national posture reflects the severity of various prison sentences to which these offenders are often subjected. To suggest leniency is frequently reserved for white defendants and rarely in evidence in the judicial dispositions of many jurists for minority offenders, is to recognize the obvious reality of a collective and indiscriminate bias, which invalidates any pretensions of the notion that "justice is blind."

In a larger context the narrative of our country's commitment initially to slavery, and subsequent to the Civil War, in a process of racism, particularly virulent regarding the welfare of our African American population in the South, has been either explicitly supported, implicitly ignored, or tolerated by many among those Caucasians who have are residents of these regions. More recently, those white males who have been stranded by the withdrawal of companies from rural areas and urban factories, and have in the absence of retraining programs or educational assistance themselves become members of the American poverty class, often embrace these prejudices.

For the approximately 60 million of our citizens who are imprisoned in impoverishment, as well as the overwhelming majority of their children, the "American Dream" is deceased. Their prospects are grim and brutal, and they are often forgotten and discarded by those of us who, in our daily travels, rarely interact with these individuals as we wend our way from relatively comfortable homes to tolerable offices and factories, and other facilities where our economy continues to function. For the "working poor," i.e. those who can be found toiling away at companies such as McDonalds and Walmart and other chain store operations in both the U.S. and globally, franchisees often manipulate schedules to insure overtime compensation is never warranted. In addition, healthcare is virtually non-existent for these employees of various sub-contractors, work weeks in excess of fifty hours are common, and frequently those who are given the option of an occasional respite from work are asked to be prepared if various contingencies develop, to be in an "on-call" status.

The minimum wages provided to these employees are wholly insufficient to support themselves and their families. In fact, these salaries are so meager these employees are encouraged to seek second employment opportunities to augment their incomes, and/or apply to federal or state programs of assistance for which they are eligible; given the horrendously inadequate pay scales they are provided. In excess of 150 billion dollars of federal aid has been provided to these employees from 2009 - 2011.

It is those in this segment of the nation's economy where the cruelest of all economic realities exist. These employees composed overwhelmingly of immigrants from Mexico, and other Latin American and South American countries, are drawn to the U.S. by the lure and possibility of converting their sweat and aptitudes, into a life of material sufficiency and upward mobility. Rarely are those aspirations actualized. As years pass and their occupational status remains marginalized and extraordinarily insecure, they continue to be subject to the whims of franchisees and the formulation of policies that derive from corporate headquarters. Frequently, with little notice or justification, these employers embark upon yet another round of cost-cutting and production efficiencies, in which the absurdly paltry wages of their employees become subject to further reductions to achieve the desired increases in revenues and, most importantly, profitability, of these conglomerates.

But what may you inquire are the circumstances of the overwhelming majority of our citizens who are not consigned to ghettos and disintegrating rural locales? Surely, their lives reflect a vibrant and a fulfilling status of contentment and financial security. To give credence to this fiction is to invalidate and demean the struggles and challenges which life in the U.S. for this group reflects. Membership in the middleclass, at this moment, is tenuous, fraught with the consistently looming threat of reductions in both work schedules and compensation.

As technology replaces human exertion and productivity, twin tragedies of displacement by these automatons and the allocation of these productivity gains to senior executives rather than those in the depleted ranks of employees result. Seniority is of little consequence as is the position within a company's table of organization which employees have been assigned. It is the primacy of exclusively market considerations that determine when and where facilities and commercial enterprises shall be located, function, and/or whose operations shall be discontinued. The constant anxieties, which these economic circumstances produce, are among the primary inhibiters that discourage employees from seeking more lucrative employment because so few exist. Moreover, the herculean efforts to obtain these positions can require months of sustained exertion and substantial expenditures of energy, and consume the precious few hours in their lives devoted to family nurturing and personal responsibilities.

The current process of securing employment is laden with a multitude of barriers to access and consideration. Software programs eliminate from review thousands of resumes that do not conform in language and precise work experience to the qualities various employers are seeking. Moreover, because so many applicants exist and are aggressively pursuing these job opportunities, these organizations frequently erect a structure of requirements that virtually no candidate possesses. Rather than sift through the dozens or, in some instances, hundreds of "qualified" candidates, these human resource executives seek prospective colleagues from among the coterie of friends and associates in their networks, thus enormously reducing the pool from which these individuals are drawn. In addition, the companionate fear their current employers may learn of their desire to obtain alternative employment and be punitive in their response to this knowledge, and/or provide unfavorable references to those who inquire about the character or competence of this individual, frequently inhibits their job search.

As a result, there is little incentive among major corporations to either expand their workforce or provide greatly deserved wage increases that reward employees for their efforts even when, in many instances, their contributions result in improved and more cost-effective production processes, and/or other operational or administrative innovations that find their way to an augmented bottom-line.

Should those in their employ become disgruntled what alternatives for their services exist? Very few. Should they, nonetheless, withdraw from these positions replacing them will present very little challenge, given the current universe of those in this nation who are currently unemployed, underemployed, and receiving few if any benefits, or are recipients of compensation tantamount to the minimum wage in their respective communities. These macro-economic factors and the stress and insecurities they represent are most effective tools in creating and sustaining a compliant and apprehensive population. Moreover, domestic and personal responsibilities preclude the devotion of any meaningful periods of time or effort to engage as citizens with the political process and/or other non-governmental organizations. Their schedules of professional and familial obligation preclude their support of initiatives to mitigate or rectify these legitimate grievances, or create a society in which social justice, in some meaningful regard, may be observed.

The trio of exhaustion, an agenda of unceasing parental and marital obligations, and the apprehensions inherent in our current economic circumstances conspire to deprive so many of us of the critical requirement in a posture of leisurely exploration and examination, of evaluating whether the ethical and religious principles, which we embrace, are manifest in the social and political dimensions of this nation's cultural reality.

In the U.S., a very broad spectrum of religious systems are operative and the gamut of theological principles extends from the Judeo-Christian precepts, Buddhist dogma, and Muslim beliefs etc. to those who have rejected any formal involvement in a system in which a Deity exists.

However, even among the latter group principally of the Millennial generation, there is a robust and authentic embrace of Humanist concepts that reflect the intrinsic value of each individual the inherent right of human beings to exist in a state of freedom, and exercise the specific personal liberties inherent in that status.

Beyond the preceding rights are those which demand we be afforded the opportunity to an educational process and safe physical environment in which to reside, as well as the provision of the material sustenance, that will permit these individuals to remain, at the very least, viable, and ultimately become more robustly self-sustaining. Thus, with the exception of a very few in our midst, virtually all of us are united in some fundamental regard, whether the moorings are found in religious texts or the works of Humanist philosophers, innate to the human condition do certain inalienable rights exist. Moreover, these principles have been enunciated and unceasingly reiterated in the founding documents that created America and in subsequent periods of unrest and agitation as we confronted the legitimate demands of those among us who had been the victims of discrimination and exclusion, from participating in some central regard in the freedoms and bountiful harvests so many of us were experiencing.

This document proceeds from the critical and non-negotiable premise our present difficulties exist because we have not, as a nation, translated those religious and ethical values we cherish and subscribe to into the overarching realities of our culture. We have, as individuals, either neglected the effort to fully render explicitly our belief systems or, in a posture of denial and impotence, have ceded this activity to others claiming the ignorance and/or inability, to comprehend and implement this imperative moral protocol.

This most virulent myth of powerlessness and lack of capacity must be irrevocably shattered by the awareness of a truth that, in the face of systematic, sustained, and collective personal engagement by the majority of our population, nothing is impossible. But, to those of you who are waiting for the candidacy of Elizabeth Warren, or the arrival of the cavalry to engage and nullify the power of undemocratic and oppressive institutions, or for those who proudly wore as did I, the uniform of a U.S. Marine during the Vietnam era, my brethren will not be dispatched to redress these grievances and restore a more just and democratic social order.

No, my fellow citizens, this task falls to all of us if we are to recreate an America that embodies the religious requirements and humanistic prescriptions to which we ostensibly pledge our fealty, as well as the political precepts undergirded the establishment of this country 239 years ago.

In subsequent chapters of this work, I shall address what, in my view, is the nature and content of those activities which possess the potential to transform this nation. But, know this: in the absence of a national commitment to rectify these deplorable economic and social realities, this prospective effort shall not succeed.

Beyond the tactic of onerous work schedules, lengthy commutes, the perpetuation of inherently insecure job tenure, and the cumulative toll this physical and psychic exhaustion exacts on our capacities to examine and evaluate the content of our lives and the injustices extant in our nation, and the ultimate ability to formulate those crucial responses to achieve greater equality and social justice, is the second element of a continuing massive tsunami of data and information, which the birth of the Internet has created.

Beyond the electronic media, the fourth estate, other weekly or monthly publications in this the era of the email and the blog, and the elevation of significant numbers of our citizens to the role of self-appointed political and social commentator, as well, the magnitude of information to which we are subject has expanded geometrically in the past two decades. Moreover, each sub-component that appears on the ideological continuum has become ever more insular and dogmatic in its perspectives, and increasingly deletes from its menu any voices or views which contradict its values. Thus, are those who suffer from extreme fatigue and gnawing apprehension about so much in their lives, are flooded with twenty-four hour news cycles, cable television's incessant drum beat of disclosure, tidal waves of articles on the Internet from dozens of outlets and providers consisting of advice and autobiographical vignettes that frequently have but tangential relevance to our challenges and issues.

In addition, the continuous receipt of spam entries that offer products and services to tantalize our pocketbooks and awaken desires of which we were previously unaware, and of course the unending stream of emails from friends, associates, acquaintances, and those with whom we are almost totally unfamiliar, to keep us apprised of all the developments in their lives, however banal or insignificant, continues in its increasing volume and upward trajectory. Our focus is distracted. We are overwhelmed by so much that is trivial and irrelevant to the flourishing of our better selves and our capacities to be compassionate toward the plight of our fellow citizens.

The fundamental nature of what is transmitted on this modality is about self-absorption, material acquisition, the perpetual quest to become slimmer, more attractive and virile, and exude a powerful sexual attractiveness to the objects of our lust. The controversies and conflict often presented concern matters that bear little relation to those concerns with which we, as Americans, should be examining, i.e. economic opportunity, inequality, the continuing degradation of our cultural literacy and the impoverishment of our public educations systems. Instead, they address, in sarcastic tones and demeaning vocabularies, the behavior of celebrities and feuds that are superficial, and reflect selfishness in which their lives are immersed. Welcome to the era of the ascendancy of gossip and insignificance.

Beyond the preceding, perhaps, what is the most grievous aspect of this dynamic prevalent in reality shows and recent cable television offerings is the general coarsening of our moral sensibilities and altruistic predispositions. Moreover, the obsession by which many of our youth our bewitched, i.e. werewolves and vampires is truly a phenomenon that calls into question their capacity for rational analysis.

The lamentable fact that the viewing public has become so invested in the debates and controversies surrounding these meaningless discussions their essence has undergone a metamorphism, and serves a displacement function; a national psychic and intellectual sublimation of those substantive matters that should occupy their lives and consciousness. However, rarely are these topics broached and rhetorically ventilated because many of our citizens have become alienated from the political process by virtue of its capture by an oligarchy, and are of the tragic opinion its remediation lies beyond their individual and collective capacities. Thus, they channel their rage and sullen discontent about our society's current circumstances into those disputes that, by virtue of their superficiality and confined dimensions, provide them with the opportunity to register an impact on the dialogue and join in a collective chorus of approbation or denunciation.

Beyond exhaustion and a surfeit of data, is our national obsession with sports franchises that annually compete for our attention and our expenditures, in such areas as baseball, football, hockey, soccer, basketball, tennis, and track and field events. Among those that appear on this calendar, are the annual rivalries among our nation's most prestigious universities and colleges in search of the Holy Grail of national championships, NCAA titles, other awards of enormous significance, and, of course, on a quadrennial basis such contests as the Olympics and the World Cup.

Do I condemn those rabid sports fans? Of course not. I have been known to agonize over the plight, particularly of my beloved New York Yankees; a team my father introduced to me many decades ago as a child living in Manhattan. I was mesmerized by the majesty of Yankee Stadium from the instant I set foot in that arena. However, when added to burdens which stress creates, and attempting to remain au courant with the torrents of electronic data and the comprehensive range of program offerings innumerable channels present, our various obsessions with the success and failure of these teams and their exploits, further distracts us from the matter of devoting virtually any time, energy, or consciousness to the examination of our lives and our national circumstances. Of course, that is precisely the point and intention of those who sit astride our hegemonic corporate institutions; to create a populace insecure financially, drowning in data and information, and further distracted by the fortunes of teams we attach our respective loyalties. Their companionate hope is awash in fads and trends, continually encouraged to lust after luxury possessions, and to acquire the respect and admiration of our associates and friends by accumulating the status these badges of wealth and privilege confer, nothing of cognitive substance will be possible.

These lives are committed to feverish activity, acquisition, and unceasing accomplishment. In those states of engagement with the challenges and demands on our resources, physical and mental, they presuppose an examined life and a deliberate agenda and chronology, if implemented, would provide the truly central achievement of a rich, rewarding existence, is not possible to conceive or implement.

The existence to which I am referring in its intrinsic character is concerned with mutually rewarding friendships and associations, and a recurring immersion in the beauty of nature, the extraordinary solace and comfort and joy art, music, and other creative forms of human activity furnish in enriching our soul.

It is the further understanding that all of us within the human community are indivisibly linked and our collective welfare and enjoyment of our various planetary journeys, which our moral values and global institutions afford, greatly transcends in importance the assets and efficacy of an infinitesimal group of individuals. By their current behaviors, these plutocrats preclude the possibility of realizing a life in which personal self-actualization, spiritual growth, and, at its center, a source of joy, pleasure, and fulfillment for all those who do not share membership in this statistically rarefied assemblage of the elite, and perhaps most ironically in a posture of self-imposed masochism, themselves as well.

The associated costs and expenditures in financial and human terms of these current social arrangements as the unbroken ascendancy of an arc that reflects such pathologies as cancer, cardiovascular ailments, elevated blood pressure, respiratory afflictions, diabetes, and a host of other impairments. For many of us to cope with the pressures and demands of this system, tranquilizers, anti-depressants, anti-anxiety medications, and sleeping aids become the pharmacological prerequisites to function. The combined expenditures for these drugs exceed approximately $300 billion annually.

In further support of the maintenance of the structure of the American social organism, a phalanx of mental health professionals, therapists, analysts, psychologists, psychiatrists, and counselors attempt to preach the gospel of accommodation, realism, adjustment, and conformity to the "realities" we find ourselves culturally immersed within. Rarely, do these agents of counsel to the aggrieved among us advocate liberation from these social institutions, or identify resources or organizations in this nation that might assist those for whom life has become so onerous and stultifying, to create an alternative way of being for themselves and their families.

Therapy for this group who specialize in healing the angst and suffering of those with mental health challenges is almost always an exercise in "anger management" when there is much in our society legitimately worthy of rage. In addition, this universe of patients is exhorted to practice "acceptance" of those values and institutions and their influences and behavior, however inimical to our spiritual and psychological evolution and contentment these dynamics may be. Should they fail in these attempts to convince us, they will finally advocate the acknowledgment these forces are beyond our personal and collective ability to rectify, resist, or transform, and to engage in such efforts is a futile exercise in torment and masochism, and augurs a certain result of failure and devastating emotional consequences. So much for the exalted prescriptions of Abraham Maslow, Carl Rogers, Paul Goodman, and others who, in postures of humanistic self-actualization, insisted in order for the human community to achieve a status that was liberating and afforded the continual ability to transcend our current limitations and entrapments, social institutions must become infinitely more elastic. So too should these entities be susceptible to the alterations and structural reconstruction that will allow individuals to engage in a perpetual exercise in unceasingly becoming citizens whose twin abilities of personal growth and an equally vivid concern for the welfare of our larger national community remains the most important objectives to which we are as a nation committed.

Finally, let us consider social media. We, as a nation, are further alienated from so much in our country that would previously unite and animate us in activities that required us to join with our neighbors and friends in the celebration of life, which only these involvements with mutual interactions and collective participation, organic in character, could afford. From these events, contests, and joint efforts, the fabric of a caring and empathetic national consciousness was created and sustained throughout so much of our history.

Today, tragically, much of that has been eroded, and many of us clutch the ever-present I-Phone, and similar devices, maintaining a dialogue with our friends and associates through the medium of texting.

On such platforms as Twitter, Facebook, and other such sites where abbreviated messages often of 140 characters or less, reduce communication to hastily authored vignettes and status reports on people's lives, relationships, impending agendas, as well as frequently sarcastic and critical observations of others in their circle of cohorts are our constant electronic companions. Once again, it is this circle of endlessly proliferating data and the forfeiture of the scant schedule of uncommitted moments during our day to these technological imprisonments that reduce our critical intellectual capacities and the time these matters might be examined, and crucial decisions about our lives and our nation could be formulated.

Among the preceding itinerary of distractions are video games that are brutal and violent in bloodshed of unceasing combat. In addition, the menu of selections beyond military and/or criminal activities is the ever-exploding genre of highly sexualized videos and, beyond that frontier, innumerable options within the world of pornography whatever one's preference for partners and circumstances.

The cumulative result of all these influences is the continuing diminishment of virtually all of our citizens, the corresponding decrease in attention spans, and the crucial ability to engage in the most important requirement for an informed citizenship, i.e. the ability to think critically. Cultural literacy is decreasing dramatically, and though extraordinary expenditures have been allocated to improving the capacity of systems and teachers in K-12 public schools, by states and the federal government, in recent decades our profile of national educational accomplishments among our students continues its comparative decline vis-a-vis other nations student bodies' at these levels.

Though there is much public discussion and great concern among our civic leaders, public servants, and educators about these developments, little of substance has been undertaken to effectively redress these deplorable circumstances. The principal twin obstructions are many teachers unions adamantly oppose the abolition of tenure and, more importantly, the notion of dismissing incompetent teachers, regardless of their length of service, and vehemently resist the expansion of charter schools and other experiments that have begun to produce improved results regarding literacy and mathematical capabilities.

However, even more important to the maintenance of the status quo, i.e. failure and at best mediocrity, is the fact those who sit at the apogee of our economic pinnacle are not overly disturbed about the current public education realities for a nation whose populace lacks the tools and skills to think critically and engage as informed and intellectually competent adults in our political dialogue, is infinitely more manageable. Moreover, in concert with all that coexists in our society regarding the character and profusion of innumerable distractions, these individuals will remain compliant and susceptible to ideological manipulation and social interpretations often deceptive, dishonest, reflect misdirection, and, on occasion, are blatant lies and preposterous fabrications that justify the current social and political order.

This community of infinitesimal elites is content to permit and, in some de facto regard, encourage the maintenance of the status quo as the result of another highly important consideration. Their children have access to infinitely richer and more sophisticated educational environments that can be found in very expensive private schools and academies Upon graduation, the option of attending the most prestigious colleges and universities awaits them, and in those settings where the Humanities and Social Sciences remain central elements of their curricula to learn precisely those methodologies and approaches to the mastery of various complex and imperative disciplines, to sharpen their cognitive skills and powers of critical intellectual evaluation. Subsequent to completing their undergraduate studies at these schools, many acquire MBA's, law degrees, or Ph.D.'s where they deploy in their careers frequently at investment banks, hedge funds, and consulting and law firms the very skills and talents their parents have utilized effectively in maintaining, for yet another generation, the perpetuation about much of our nation's current reality that is antidemocratic, unjust, and morally reprehensible.

The Role Which Consumer Debt/Financial Obligations Incurred In The Higher Education Process Serves

Beyond the preceding array of negative influences, i.e. psychological stress, financial insecurity, globalization, technological innovation, and the principal beneficiaries of those productivity increases, e.g. senior executives, shareholder dividends, stagnating wages, and the ever ascending requirements of various credentials and degrees for employment, additional negative variables exist.

Coexisting with these factors is an enormously seductive capacity of awarding to those who are employed and have demonstrated the responsible use of credit instruments, the ability to acquire a minute portion of the material "American Dream." Whether it's Visa or MasterCard, American Express or the Discover card, or, in many instances for those whose credit ratings are marginal or unsatisfactory, those credit instruments when fees interest rates and/or associated costs are tantamount to a cumulative expense level which borders on the usurious, are obtainable. Thus, it becomes possible for many Americans to indulge their lust for the labels and trademarks that symbolize status and affluence t]those advertising and marketing agencies constantly trumpet, in their quest to seduce ever more purchases and achieve inroads in previously inaccessible market segments. Sneakers with multi-colored laces, cupcakes incomparable in taste and cost, the next generation of technological devices, autos equipped with so many features they require ever diminishing human involvement, films that are the sequels of sequels all infantile and awash in violence and sexual imagery and entirely removed from the content of our reality. In addition, pay-per-view events that focus on wrestling matches where outcomes are scripted and villains and heroes continually alternate as those in attendance, at these arenas and in the viewing audience, grow weary of a champion's tenure or long for new faces, for which they can jeer, are within reach of their remote controls.

Vacations on cruise lines are ever more abbreviated and costly, tours and attractions are hollow and/or where cruelty to animals, which perform in these shows, be they aquatic in setting or in a circus environment may be glimpsed. Time and space constraints do not permit a further exploration of these possible options and involvements; suffice it to say the menu from which we select is unending and exceedingly comprehensive. Thus, given our human frailties we often succumb to these temptations and in our wish to experience a sense of commercial potency and be among the first wave of trend setters, do we consume our credit line, and by so doing incur debt and in many instances this debt is substantial, and completely depletes our further ability to incur additional debt, until the current obligations are reduced.

Often interest charges are significant and given the limited resources to which most of us have access the discretionary ability to discharge this debt is modest, and often requires many months of frugality and a discipline to ensure we remain current with our obligations, lest our credit ratings founder and we find ourselves the target of collection agencies and their not so tender mercies. Moreover, once we have forfeited our standings regarding the responsible use of credit, the time and effort required to repair these ratings and return to the good lending graces of various banks and credit unions, can require months if not years of effort and sacrifice.

Unless these debts are discharged in some manner agreeable to the lender, the possibility of obtaining loans for college, the purchase of autos or homes, to establish a business or acquire various consumer goods and products, will be severely curtailed.

In the final analysis, these loans, though they provide a modest access to indulge our whims and desires and provide momentary membership in the ranks of those who are viewed as influential and important in this society, demand our continued commitment to employment circumstances that are dreary, monotonous, and over which an employee exercises little if any control. Thus, consumer debt is yet another tool to ensure we remain engaged in this economy and in our present circumstances, lacking meaningful options and mired in our continually eroding median incomes that augur our fall from the middleclass, to an ever more disturbing and financially emaciated future for us and our families.

The Plight of the Millennial Generation
and Others Who Acquire a College Degree and Massive Debt

The millennial generation is departing from various institutions of higher learning in this nation, armed with credentials acquired by effort, and intellectual exertion, and unprecedented indebtedness.

Beyond the comparatively minor magnitude of debt amassed by indulging their proclivities to consume, which are made possible by banks offering credit cards with little or no assurances that these students are either employed or have demonstrated patterns of responsible and thus credit-worthy behavior, these teenagers frequently incur loan obligations for vacations, frequent visits to expensive restaurants and pubs, elegant and expensive apparel and other luxuries. Should they default on these repayments and their credit ratings are imperiled, their parents intervene to prevent their children from the significant and negative financial consequences, which can impact their access to a career trajectory or, in some instances, entry to any professional employment environment.

This frivolous and self-indulgent use of these credit instruments further encourages their desires to become ever more involved in the transactions of our consumer society and committed to the pursuit of careers that will enable them to live in luxurious surroundings and enjoy a life of comfort and ease. Irrespective of the costs to their moral sensibilities and the sacrifice of the meaningful expression of their individualistic talents and persona, which those corporate and financial institutional behemoths demand of their employees, they proceed blithely to undertake these financial responsibilities.

However, it is usually not debt incurred for personal consumption and pleasure that comprise the major portion of the financial obligations with which these graduates and frequently those who do not graduate, but have been engaged in the unsuccessful pursuit of degrees are saddled with as they drive away from these campuses on lovely spring mornings. No, these debts are of a wholly different magnitude and are currently approaching approximately $30 thousand per student. In those instances where graduate education, law, medical, and doctoral degrees are conferred, the range of debt can total in excess of $250 thousand.

In some instances, given the dearth of jobs that exist and the huge numbers of unemployed seeking these positions, the current unemployment rate for the millennial cohort exceeds 10% of those who have obtained college degrees. In those instances where GED's or high school diplomas reflect the final level of educational achievement, it is 25%. Moreover, those entry-level jobs provide wage scales that are far from generous and many recent graduates find themselves in unpaid intern situations for significant periods of time, before a salaried position becomes accessible.

The difficulty of supporting oneself on these incomes is enormously challenging and, in many instances, approximately one third of these young adults find themselves taking up residence in their parents' basements to conserve scarce resources, while attempting to develop a schedule of repayment to those lending institutions that provided the funds for their collegiate journey. As the result of these factors, marriage is delayed, home ownership is not possible, independence, in some instances from the assistance and encouragement of their parents, does not occur until their thirties or beyond, and the matter of child bearing in this segment of our population is deferred as well. Among those who are high school graduates, marriage is declining in importance and frequency, and more young people in this age category are bringing children into this world outside of wedlock.

To those of you who may object to the characterization of describing the responsible repayment of incurred debt obligation on an "as agreed" basis as a human quality negative in behavioral or moral terms, you have misconstrued the thrust of my remarks. Of course, honoring our obligations, whether financial or with regard to personal commitments to all persons/institutions is laudable and worthy conduct.

My objection relates to the fact in the service of ensnaring gullible and impressionable adolescents to become a participant in commercial transactions, which places significant obstructions on their road to personal financial viability. These interactions do nothing but deepen the messages of our society regarding material accumulation and the necessity of equating happiness with the capability to enjoy luxurious and exceedingly exclusive and invariably costly events and environments, and further increases their propensity to pursue these value systems, which worship at the altar of consumerism. Moreover, many decades ago when I was traversing the numerous hurdles that lay between myself and the accumulation of undergraduate and graduate degrees, the various programs available through state and federal sources of financial assistance were numerous and robustly funded. The interest rates and fees associated with these loans were modest indeed. The view was au courant in that timeframe was higher education success benefits, not only the individual who succeeded in his/her quest for knowledge with regard to the career access a degree presupposed, but the nation, in an important and aggregate manner, would derive great value from a population that became ever more sophisticated and intellectually accomplished.

We, as a society, would augment our cognitive and technical skills and our ability to compete with other economies, which would spur the continuous rise of our GNP, and the equally vital capacity of our citizens, to assess their personal journeys and that of this democracy, in a posture of critical examination.

In recent years, as in so many other sectors of our economy, private banking institutions became important sources of student loans as the result of arrangements with various colleges and universities which benefit these institutions financially, and the total costs of this assistance increased significantly. For these financial institutions, our student populations became another source of profitability, inflating the value of their equity shares, enriching stockholders with increased dividends, and significantly impacting those in the executive suites of these organizations by inflating their already bloated compensation packages. This process of engagement reflects the usurpation of public sources of funding which were efficient and most reasonable in terms of interest rates, a circumstance where public funds were reduced or almost entirely eliminated by Congressional Fiat, as mammoth private capital resources were substituted.

The result of this substitution increased costs significantly for the students who availed themselves of this assistance, and in the burgeoning instances where repayment became difficult or impossible for the reasons cited previously, the taxpayer was the ultimate party responsible for ensuring these loans were repatriated, and these financial institutions as a result remained viable and enormously profitable. By retaining this magnitude of profitability, they could seek other objectives domestically or internationally, in which to continue the unceasing pursuit of investments provided ever more lucrative returns regardless of the negative consequences to our nation's welfare and the ramifications relative to unprecedented inequality, which these activities support and foster.

Privatizing Traditional Activities/Services of Government at the Federal and State Echelons

In 2000, when George W. Bush sought the presidency of the U.S. he importuned Dick Cheney the CEO of Halliburton to resign his post and assist the then President-Elect in assembling a Cabinet for his impending administration. His initial task was to spearhead a formal transition process to ensure a smooth transfer of power from the departing Clinton team to the imminent ascension of Bush loyalists and ultimately, accept the Vice-Presidency in his term as the nation's Chief Executive.

Halliburton's primary areas of commercial activity were related to infrastructural projects, the provision of technical and administrative personnel that could provide a total range of services to governments and the private sector and related logistical capacities. In addition, this company's menu of services included institutional food preparation, transport, discrete construction projects for housing personnel, as well as such projects as the creation of military installations, and the entire range of those components required for their operations. Moreover, this company could furnish various sources of energy required to maintain these facilities and enable the movement of troops and other civilian personnel vital to sustain the gamut of both military and administrative activities inherent in the conduct of warfare, and in the support of associated functions necessary to maintain the governments of allies engaged in these campaigns.

Among the final acts, the Board of Directors of Halliburton ratified, immediately prior to Mr. Cheney's resignation, was to provide him with a 32 million dollar severance package as an extraordinary gift for his services as the corporation's CEO. This was a tenure which was not distinguished by any remarkable aspects of progress, or substantially increased revenues or profitability.

Not long thereafter, subsequent to the events of 9/11 and the wholly fabricated relevance/involvement of Iraq's role in these attacks, and in the equally spurious allegations that Saddam Hussein was manufacturing and stockpiling substantial caches of weapons of mass destruction, was the scope of hostilities enlarged.

The President sought the authorization from Congress to conduct military operations required to destroy Al-Qaida in their sanctuaries in Afghanistan and to institute a military campaign that included a regime change in Iraq.

From the inception of those efforts in these nations (a coalition of the willing was assembled in 2003 to commence hostilities in Iraq) to our withdrawal in 2011, our government allocated in excess of four trillion dollars, and Halliburton's participation in these combined efforts of military support/infrastructural construction etc. produced revenues for this company in excess of fifty billion dollars. Thus, became a precedent established in warfare. Previously, when we had committed our troops to combat missions in World War Two, Korea, Vietnam, and in Desert Storm military personnel and the Army Corps of Engineers had performed these functions.

The construction of bases, preparing and serving meals to our soldiers, transporting vital equipment and ammunition, and providing the required energy supplies to mount attacks and defend bases all fell under the aegis and institutional structures of the federal government.

Beyond the previous efforts, these entities also participated in various civilian aspects of governmental activities required to support the military efforts and the pacification of areas of the nation. Such services, as the provision of crucial medical, educational, and administrative, personnel to operate local and regional governance, and the indispensable function of ensuring the security of the civilian populations under their areas of responsibility, were all dispensed by Halliburton and other major contractors.

The numerous voices emanating from the executive suites of corporate towers declared this effort to "privatize" much of what had been provided in previous conflicts by military, diplomatic, or intelligence elements of our government could be contracted out to private corporations, and the results of that effort would ensure these services could be dispensed with much greater efficiency than under the government's domain. Moreover, it was their contention the cost-benefit ratios under civilian administration/operation would produce significant economies of scale, and thus, achieve the mission's manifold objectives at great savings to the American taxpayer.

When superimposed upon the reality of the experiences of Afghanistan and Iraq, the precise opposite of those assertions materialized. The cost of contracting and sub-contracting these services greatly exceeded the expenses their provision by military and civilian employees of our government would have required. The instances, in which shoddy construction, graft, and corruption involving American companies, Iraqi government officials, and other Iraqis engaged in the actual construction of these facilities under the umbrella of the reconstruction program initiated by the State Department, comprised a substantial minority of all such projects undertaken. However, it was those tragic instances security contractors were accused of the entirely unjustified use of lethal force vis-a-vis civilians' protests, created enormous strain in our relationship with the Iraqi government and the citizens of that nation, eclipsed all previous misdeeds.

In other realms of activity beyond the military "out-sourcing" responsibilities, customarily resided within public governmental or the public educational sphere preempted by private for profit companies. They currently provide such services as penal facilities construction and management, educational training, curricula formulation, teacher training seminars, administrative and operational aspects of public school facilities, and testing and counseling expertise. They are the purveyors of college preparatory and advisory programs for students and parents and, very recently, a geometric expansion of evaluation and assessment organizations to measure comparative approaches to learning in the K-12 environments. Moreover, there has been a proliferation of for profit course offerings and credentials for such skills as nursing, physicians' assistants, computer development, software and hardware design, maintenance services, and technical institutes.

These entities provide cutting edge training in technologies currently utilized in high-tech manufacturing environments, and in those programs that train auto mechanics and long distance truck drivers, to cite a few.

My concern with these opportunities is not their existence or their assisting students in creating vitally necessary capabilities for the contemporary American workplace. Rather, my objections stem from three principal realities associated with these companies.

The government funds that fuel these undertakings should be allocated to our national system of public vocational schools and community colleges, rather than to for-profit schools, whose cost is substantially greater to provide this instruction than the previously cited institutional settings. In addition, numerous complaints have been registered against some of these companies regarding the dearth of employment opportunities in the various fields students have acquired their expertise, as well as the exorbitant compensation packages the CEO's generate, which can exceed six and seven figure annual incomes.

My final source of unhappiness about these for profit institutions is when graduates of these programs are incapable of obtaining employment in these fields of endeavor and, as a result, lack the financial resources to repay the loan obligations they have assumed to enroll in these courses; many of these organizations adopt a posture of complete indifference to their plight.

The reason, these for-profit institutions are relatively unconcerned about these eventualities is they have received tuition and associated payments for their instruction, and they are not liable to either refund to the student or the loan source, the repayment of these monies, in the event a student is unsuccessful in becoming employed.

The ultimate source of repayment to these lending institutions is, of course, the federal government, when individuals, through no fault of their own, default because of a lack of suitable employment opportunities. Once again, it is the American taxpayer who must absorb the responsibility of the repayment of the debt.

Beyond the realm of government or education, we have witnessed in recent years the enlargement of the private sector's participation in such elements of the economy as the ownership and operation of railroad lines, public utilities, and toll roads.

In virtually every instance in which public ownerships has yielded to private control and functional oversight, the following pattern of reality evolves. Management rarely improves in any substantive manner the efficiency of these facilities, the compensation of senior executives is enormously increased, and the employees' incomes and perks remain stagnant and, in some instances, recede as the result of this process of privatization.

The history of the privatization of various railroad systems reflects much of what may be glimpsed in the realm of the public utilities, i.e. increased costs for services provided freight and passenger traffic customers, a reduction of frequency in the number of trains and the schedules to which they, on rare occasions, adhere. Moreover, stratospheric increments in the compensation awarded to senior executives invariably occur, and the relative emasculation of the unions, which represent their employees, are exceedingly common occurrences. These pernicious developments result in the stagnation of wages, an increase in the number of hours work schedules require, a reduction of benefits in medical insurance packages, sick leave provisions, and vacation periods, which these unionized work forces are allocated. In addition, productivity increments resulting in more profitable operations are rarely funneled to employees. Rather, these revenues find their way to shareholders in the form of elevated dividends, the repatriation of additional shares of the company's equity from public markets, and as bonuses and salary increases for those who sit at the apogee of the company's table of organization.

An egregious example of this practice occurred in the state of Indiana. The former Republican governor, Mitch Daniels, permitted a major private investment firm to acquire the ownership of a state higheway, The Indiana Toll Road. This throughfare served a portion of the state experiencing considerable congestion, which compelled longer commutes and the accompanying frustration, resulting from snarled traffic patterns, and the darkening moods of weary travelers.

Previously, when these infrastructure improvements were required in virtually every state, including Indiana, the government would issue bonds to obtain the capital to construct these roads and the tolls collected during the life of the road would repay the bond holders with a modest profit. In addition, these toll receipts provided a source of revenue to defray a portion of the state's annual expenditures to maintain and improve the state's bridges, highways, tunnels, and other transportation modalities, as well as other categorical expenditures.

In the instance cited, the funds allocated to the state government exceeded the expense incurred by the state in the construction of this thoroughfare. However, the "cost" of this arrangement with this private source of capital, was the requirement to divert from state coffers the revenue from all tolls collected, to the private entity that acquired its ownership, operations, and maintenance requirements. The results of this contractual relationship would permit this private sector entity to reap prospective revenues that were multiples of their investment, and would reflect an unprecedented return on the dollars committed. Moreover, subsequent to its acquistion tolls were increased by approximately 300%, expenditures to sustain the appropriate operations of this throughfare were significantly reduced, and funds to ensure the requisite maintance of this road were diminished. However, what compounds this tragic governmental agreement is the fact the recession of 2008 has greatly depleted the tax revenues which all governments, federal, state, and local, had acquired.

What is crucial about this continuing flow of revenue over the longer term of the toll road's life is it would provide the state with the capability to expand its services and address the requirements of many residents who, as the result of the debacle of the Great Recession, found themselves unemployed, homeless, and careening toward a life of poverty and hopelessness. Thus, does this arrangement penalize the state in the longer term by depriving it of billions of dollars to support and maintain the delivery and provision of those crucial services to a constituency in desperate need of them to survive, until their careers and lives can be restored by an as yet unrealized economic recovery.

In the previous segments of this document, I have attempted to provide a comprehensive introduction to both the principal motivations of this nation's economic royalty and the primary arenas of involvement to which they allocate a broad spectrum of resources in order to retain their hegemony over the American culture. However, it is crucial in my view to present an additional aspect of the continuum of forces that prod and provoke many of these financial elites to engage not simply to succeed in their professional endeavors, as so many of our citizens wish to, i.e. the appropriate deployment of ambition and the companionate desire to establish a personal profile of accomplishment, of which they and their families, associates and friends might regard as laudable and commendable.

Rather, is it the circumstance in this infinitesimal group of individuals that compels them to amass greater wealth and commensurate influence in this society than all others are a constellation of forces that have taken up residence in their unconsciousness and in their psyches, which demand a level of achievement and recognition exceeds the reputation and esteem in which others are held.

The psychological dynamics to which I am referring relate to such notions as self-loathing, a carefully inculcated series of messages from within the nuclear family environment frequently reflected by the practices their parents have implemented in the process of child-rearing. These influences create a conciousness within these individuals of a complete lack of intrinsic value and a sense their existences are superfluous with little meaning or relevance to the human condition.

In response to these interior normative lenses, through which they view the world and their place in it, they devote their lives, energies, and aptitudes to demonstrating to those who gave them life and to the society at large, these evaluations which have so brutally deformed and defaced their self-images are completely erroneous.

It is this ferocious compusion that fuels the imperative to realize extraordinary accomplishments within their chosen field of professional endeavor. For it is these achievements that shall refute those assessments that are negative in character and critically, support the contention their capabilities, brilliance, and magnitude of their material resources eclipses all others.

As a result, I shall devote much of the second chapter to these concerns and related considerations, which explore the psychological crucible in which they were formed and, contemporarily, reside.

CHAPTER TWO

The Psychopathology in which these Elites are Imprisoned
& the Inimical Results of Its Expression

T he conventional wisdom that abounds in this nation is those elect few who have attained great wealth and commensurate influence embody lives of extraordinary indulgence and experience a consciousness of joyous contentment. For they inhabit the rarefied atmosphere of a material paradise that insulates them from the mundane and vexing challenges which comprise so much of the content of those of us whose material resources by comparison are meager, stagnating, or declining.

We are of the virtually unanimous opinion this group of CEO's who comprise the Forbes 400 who are experiencing lives of unparalleled accomplishment, and who reside at the epicenter of an orbit of professional associates and reverential acolytes, must have acquired a peace, joy, and an enormous sense of fulfillment few others have known. However, for the vast majority of those who occupy those exalted locales at the pinnacle of these corporate and financial institutions, a quite different and in fact regrettable dynamic characterizes the fundamental essence of their awareness. Many of them who have devoted extraordinary effort in their quest to become CEO's of these corporate behemoths, or in postures of a rabid entrepreneurialism have created companies that through their unrelenting efforts now reign supreme in their respective areas of commercial activity, are propelled toward these heights as the result of enormous insecurities and nuclear family pathologies.

These disease syndromes have produced self-images that are deformed and reflect a primary sensibility of self-loathing, and an unremitting sense of inadequacy and deficiencies that often relate to physical characteristics of homely countenances, diminutive stature, and anemic or corpulent, physiognomies. Thus, what frequently fuels their desire to succeed is the transcendent need to demonstrate to detractors their assessments of their abilities were flawed, and their predictions of failure or mediocre destinies were in error.

In the final analysis, their vindication will be derived from their triumph to amass personal fortunes exceed those other plutocrats, who are also engaged in the ruthless and all-consuming exertions to ascend to an ever more rarefied status on the Holy Grail of annual financial rankings, the Forbes 400. It is these rankings, in their view, which will demonstrate to other captains of industry and the general public the accomplishments they are responsible, and thus empirically demonstrate to all their superiority and the incomparable qualities they represent and embody.

The crucial question, which must be posed at this juncture, is as the result of expending herculean energy and virtually every waking moment of their consciousness in the pursuit of these financial objectives, when they have achieved their goals and reside virtually alone on the apex of Mount Olympus, do they then experience a sensibility that is joyous, passionate, or creative? Are their lives populated with loving family relationships and substantive and rewarding sources of friendship that nourish their capacities to become empathetic, selfless, compromising, and affectively vibrant (all of which are required to create and sustain mutually beneficial human arrangements)?

Regrettably, in most instances, they assuredly do not experience that marvelous eventuality. For those who are compelled to demonstrate their fundamental self-worth, and by the accumulation of wealth, the traits of solipsism, self-absorption, narcissism, and obsessive-compulsive behaviors, reign supreme. So, too, do the qualities of arrogance, contempt, and condescension, become ever more entrenched and preeminent, as the central hallmarks of their consciousness and behavior. Continuing forays into episodes of alcoholic and pharmacological excess to anesthetize the isolation and boredom and emptiness of life in their palatial but sterile residences, recur with frequent regularity.

Often in the quest to resuscitate a meaningful and substantial sensorial dynamic, repetitive immersion in sadomasochistic sexual practices in which orgasmic and violent rituals commingle are recurring requisite activities. However, the most tragic and cruel irony about the lives of those who are committed to this mode of existence is regardless of the magnitude of wealth they acquire, it is never sufficient to satisfy their appetites or silence the insatiable demons that reside in their consciousness.

It is patently impossible in the material realm to achieve the conversion of a state of frantic desperation and alienation into a consciousness in which serenity, agape, and the joy of a leisurely immersion in human fellowship, emerges. Moreover, the profound yearnings and self-exploration of the wounds and vulnerabilities of an experiential compilation, in the past and current segments of their life, will continue to elude them as well in this physical environment.

The conversion of which I speak can only be accomplished through either spiritual or psychological processes. It is within the clinical realm the arduous efforts to confront and neutralize their pernicious, false, and horribly negative self-perceptions, is achieved. This accomplishment is secured with the continuing assistance of a skilled therapist, initially in exploring the content of the individuals unconscious where these atrocious messages and warped notions reside.

These communiques of misinformation have frequently been placed there over decades of reiteration, by parents who have sustained substantial scarring and cognitive deformities, as the result of the nuclear family environment in which they were reared. Subsequent to this investigation are attempts at behavioral modification implemented to remediate the self-destructive patterns of activity in which these individual are ensnared.

In the absence of a successful intervention by clinicians or by continuing immersion in a program of spiritual enlightenment, the intergenerational transmission of pathologies continues ad nauseam, ad infinitum. However, within such spiritual practices, as those found in twelve step fellowships, ever-lengthening sobriety often produces beyond abstinence from drug or alcohol use, a mentality of substantial and warranted self-regard.

It is, as the result, of the implementation of these steps in daily behavioral actions, the cognitive alternations which are possible by the retrieval of sanity, and the crucial task of invoking the assistance of a capability which transcends their personal resources, that this spiritual transformation is enabled. In addition, it is by the application of these modalities the toxicity of self-loathing is supplanted by the awareness we are deserving of self-esteem, intrinsically by virtue of our inherent status as sentient beings.

In concert with this awareness, is the recognition our conduct has been transformed from exploitive, manipulative, narcissistic, contemptuous, and self-absorbed to a pattern of interacting with others customarily considerate of their priorities and concerns. Moreover, this interpersonal modality reflects a continuing desire to be of service to our fellows in a selfless manner, seeking no recompense other than the recognition these acts of kindness produce an extraordinary sense of well-being and contentment, within them, which far exceeds the pleasure they derive from any efforts predicated on self-seeking or ego inflation.

The fundamental truth of the human experience is the sublime irony that the greatest happiness we can experience is attributable, not to those efforts which seek as their objective the augmentation of rewards or accomplishments for ourselves, but are derived from the actions we undertake to assist our fellow human beings. Those attempts to mitigate the suffering they are experiencing, whatever its causes, and augment their opportunities to live fulfilling and meaningful existences is the primary source of our contentment. It is in these acts salvation and self- transcendence can be found beyond all other locations in the human experience.

Unfortunately, the preceding enumeration of the actions of these sociopathic personalities to achieve redemption and self-worth, through the accumulation of massive wealth, comprises but a fraction of the heinous damage and misery throughout so much of this nation's social expanse, which their collective and concerted political and economic agendas produce when implemented.

Since the Reagan hegemony, the financial sector of our economy has swollen to unprecedented fund magnitudes. Investment bankers, and hedge fund managers, invest trillions of dollars annually to derive in excess of 40% of all profits realized by U.S. companies from these transactions. Most prevalent are those that exploit the minute value disparities between various sovereign currencies. However, these profits are entirely detached from any social purpose, such as the construction of factories, infrastructure rehabilitation, and the creation or enlargement of the manufacture of products or the provision of consumer or industrial services expansion. The principal beneficiaries of these commercial activities are occupants of the most affluent 1% of our economy. Moreover, graduates from Ivy-League universities who have demonstrated great competence in the realm of quantitative modeling and other technical and mathematical and economic capacities, are recruited to formulate sophisticated algorithms traders on Wall Street deploy in their never ending quest to maximize the profits obtained on the sale of derivatives and arbitrage transactions. In addition, investment offerings containing housing portfolios that relieved the issuers of virtually their entire financial obligation should market forces reflect the diminishment of their value, were enormously popular on Wall Street in the period immediately prior to our recent financial crisis.

It was this constellation of the previous activities that were among the principal culprits responsible for the horrendous negative impact on our economy during the 2008 Great Recession. Though these moguls ceaselessly proclaim the imperative necessity of sustaining the operation of free markets and the companionate necessity of reducing regulatory interference in the functioning of these financial systems and processes; their army of lobbyists ensure whatever revision of federal tax codes are introduced their obligations to provide this revenue is mitigated by exemptions from its enforcement.

As the result of the global actions of these corporations, tax liabilities are reduced in many instances to virtually zero, yet their treasuries in foreign nations contain net profits of trillions of dollars from their global operations, which they refuse to repatriate because of the "excessive" levels of taxation this transfer to American financial institutions would presuppose.

This pattern of resistance continues to occur as our anemic and essentially jobless recovery from the debacle of 2008 is exacerbated by the intransigence of Tea Party activists, who obstruct all legislative initiatives which seek to provide funds for the creation of jobs and the rehabilitation of much of our public infrastructure, continues its decline and decomposition.

Legislative initiatives emanating from either source of our bicameral legislature in any manner reduces the current advantages or future prospects of these corporate entities are usually disposed of in committee, rarely to find their way to the floor of the House or Senate for consideration. Should prospective regulatory policies be forthcoming from the federal bureaucracy that inimically impacts their operations, Cabinet secretaries and the White

House will be bombarded by a phalanx of lobbyists, who shall communicate their displeasure about the standards their clients shall be held accountable, and the costs required to affect these improvements.

Within these phone calls and emails of fierce displeasure, these representatives of our corporate elite remind the President and his senior aides, in the absence of the finaicial contributioons of their employeers, the incumbents period of residence at 1600 Pennsylvania Avenue would not have been possible.

The Tragic and Ultimate Costs to the Citizens
of the U.S. which the Hegemony of these Elites Exacts

In recent years, the incidents of tragedy in the lives of our population have increased substantially. We read or are informed by electronic media of those situations where, because of the mental instability of various individuals, they embark on horrific episodes of violence and destruction, often leaving in their gruesome wake the corpses of those whose lives they have extinguished.

In schools and universities in Colorado, Connecticut, and Virginia, the deranged among us for grievances that are the product of a hallucinatory dynamic, seek to redress these "injustices" and wreak fatal havoc on those who, from their insane perspective, deserve lethal acts of retaliation for their "crimes." That these circumstances are morally catastrophic and, of course, irreparable in their finality, and subsequent to these horrendous events do we as a nation invariably engage in a conversation about where the institutional responsibility resides in this society, beyond the culprit who was responsible for these grotesque deeds, as we should and must. However, the magnitude of the damage they inflict on our society pales in comparison when we superimpose on these events, the severity of the suffering on the lives of so many who currently reside in our nation, inflicted by those who reside at the apogee of our contemporary economic and political arrangements.

What is patently absurd about these realities is the individuals who seek enormous wealth and power in order to assuage their sense of personal inadequacy and self-loathing, were created in a nuclear family environment by parents who themselves were damaged by similar self-perceptions, by the ascendant value system, which this society has espoused for generations. Many who have become billionaires were reared in homes whose parents lived modest lives and held middleclass positions or, in other instances, existed in environments of financial deprivation.

As a result, their concerns were primarily focused on the educational opportunities their children might be afforded, in the unassailable belief from these process of socialization and intellectual accomplishment, careers of substance and affluence were attainable for them.

Lest the reader has concluded I oppose social mobility and ambition and a life devoted to professional achievement, you would be entirely in error. At the heart of the American normative structure, is the promise of self-improvement in one's social standing and financial circumstances proudly displayed. Moreover, that these opportuntiies will be improved by dint of personal effort and the application of one's energy, has historically been a commitment made to those who dwell here, and it is among many factors that distinguishes us from many other cultures in a manner that is redemptive and exemplary.

To rise from one's humble beginnings and through individual exertion achieve a significantly improved life and financial capabilities as a result, is to be applauded and is a characteristic of this nation I should most fervently wish to perpetuate and broaden to include each of us who are current residents.

My quarrel is not with these precepts, but rather the ramifications for this society when these goals are pursued with ferocity and an unbridled intention of rising above all others in the accumulation of financial assets. My further objection relates to the efficacy that flows from reality in terms of the impact and virtually unrestricted influence may be exerted, to create and sustain the current climate of "investment capitalism," that benefits few and is catastrophic to many.

For it is in this iteration beyond all other forms of a capitalist economy, that so negatively penalizes the fortunes and prospects of so many, whose lives are restricted and diminished by the absence of adequate financial resources and opportunities.

The fervent universal desire to live lives free from the anxieties that plague their psyches, which the instability of their careers and incomes has produced, is our citizens' utmost concern. Our fellow countrymen also yearn to translate the covenant between this government and the individual citizen consummated 239 years into a fully actualized reality for all those who dwell on our shores.

Are plutocrats unaware of the current economic circumstances of all who are not billionaires? Of course not. However, it is the very structure of their pathology which inures them to the suffering and anxieties which the stagnation of incomes and the innate insufficiency of them in the universe of the "working poor," create.

The tragic central reality is in their frantic quest to demonstrate those who have characterized them as deficient, as inadequate, as lacking in those qualities required to succeed in this society's commercial competition are incorrect, and their estimates and evaluations are flawed and in grievous error, have the qualities of compassion and empathy become casualties.

Inherent in these personality structures and their efforts to demonstrate their uniqueness and superlative talents in a consciousness of complete self-absorption and self-interest, is the almost total lack of sensitivity to others in human circumstances of great angst and extraordinary discomfort which they are experiencing, principally in the realm of the depletion of their financial resources.

Beyond the fact of total self-immersion, is an equally prominent dynamic that operates in their psyches which is the imperative necessity in order to experience any sense of value, is the requirement to view all others as inferior in terms of lacking various attributes and capabilities, and therefore worthy of the contempt and condescension they are regarded. Thus, from these twin platforms of self-loathing and the concomitant judgment those in this society, particularly the impoverished, are contemptible because of their individual failure to surmount poverty, educational deficiencies, or nuclear family dysfunction, and therefore don't deserve our empathy or assistance.

This moral callousness, this absence of empathy or compassion for the welfare of others and their companionate concerns and interests, is what precludes this oligarchy from a course of action internal to their corporate domains, of increasing the wages of their employees to provide access to a comfortable middle class existence. Nor in their view are these subordinate colleagues worthy of membership on the board of directors, where the company's strategic vision and operational processes are formulated and consistently reevaluated, though it is as a result of their toil these objectives come to fruition, surely their perspectives and priorities should be considered. Apparently not!

To those who suggest these entities are legally required to maximize their profits to shareholders, my response is twofold. The general levels of profitability within the private sector among fortune 500 corporations have attained unprecedented levels of profitability in their recovery from the Great Recession. Moreover, and more importantly, to consider one's employees as dispensable and nothing other than an expense incurred in the provision of the company's portfolio of products and services, is in some fundamental context to disregard their human status and all that flows from that in terms of our obligations to them, as a result.

Virtually, every system of theology advocates this ethical perspective, which can also be found at the center of Humanist values, as well as the primary obligation in the social contract we have committed as a society to honor, for all who are citizens. In addition, rarely if ever has litigation resulted because the shareholders of a corporation were displeased about the fact the wages provided to the average employee were exorbitant. Rather, it is the recognition of many enlightened CEO's in this nation, to provide adequate compensation for all those who are engaged in furnishing the skill, and talent, and energy, enables these entities to function and be profitable, are entitled to derive incomes on which they and their families may live comfortably, and participate in the enrichment as shareholders these companies accomplish.

Increasingly, corporations are appointing representatives of their work force to their Boards of Directors, and in recognition of their indispensable role in the company's operations these employees play, provide them substantial compensation packages that include stock options etc.

This modus operandi benefits all who are involved with the organization's exertions and reflects an enlightened and evolved capitalism, in its intrinsic essence manifests the values of our religious legacies and the requirements of an operational Humanism and simultaneously, honors our political obligations regarding economic opportunity to those who reside in this nation. However, though the reader may nod in vigorous agreement these concerns are morally impeccable and, in some idealized universe, were they at the helm of these companies would most surely implement these practices, they possess no such power, and thus this ethical fantasy no matter how laudable lies beyond their influence.

The facts, however, are very different. Though it is true individual citizens in and of themselves do not possess the power to persuade these organizations to reflect in their operations and employment practices equitable principles, a united populace committed to these objectives does. In addition to the previous considerations, we must demand they honor their inherent obligations to the welfare of the communities, in which they reside, and the universal imperative of eliminating those external effects for which they are responsible, that contribute to the further destruction of our planetary environment.

What we may lack as individuals, as a nation of more than 320 million we most assuredly have within our grasp, i.e. the tools and technologies to compel these critical normative and logistical alterations in these commercial enterprises.

The previous era of evaluating the activities which were permissible and required of corporate entities in the American experience, must be abolished and replaced with standards and obligations beyond the narrow world of those who currently profit extraordinarily from the current operations of an "Investment Capitalism."

This is a society whose median income is no greater than it was in 1989, and which since 2009 has decreased in excess of 7% of its value and where those whose names appear on the Forbes 400 list of wealthiest Americans, reflect an asset base that exceeds the total material resources of approximately 180 million of our least affluent citizen.

This is a nation where 60 million of our citizens are imprisoned in poverty and racism remains a virulent and negative force in many communities. Where educations systems are failing virtually everywhere in our country, and where the middleclass continues to experience the stagnation of their incomes, and the corresponding corrosion of their wealth. Moreover, this is a culture in which escalating levels of stress, anxiety, fear, and insecurity gnaw at our psyches and diminish our collective tranquility. As a result, many of us seek the refuge of both illicit and legally obtainable drugs and exotic alcoholic beverages to anesthetize our apprehension and emotional discomfort. We also live in a commonweal where the legacies of previous American foreign adventures throughout the globe have conspired with the misadventures of other former colonial European powers and regional despots to deny access to a life of self-determination and financial self-sufficiency to many on this planet.

These realities, when combined with the fanatical and psychotic stimuli of the Muslim Jihadists, is continuing to broaden the geographical scope and the destructiveness of those conflicts which abound in Syria, Iraq, Lebanon, Jordan, Turkey, and, of course, as their mutual enmity, the most salient characteristics the Israeli-Palestinian dispute reflects. As we are tragically aware, our homeland has not been spared the violent outbursts and devastating results of these ideologies and the acts of terrorists who have inflicted great loss of life.

The trauma and often irreparable damage to thousands of families who experienced the shock and excruciating sudden departure of their loved ones on that beautiful autumn day the 11th of September 2001, and subsequent to that during a recent running of the Boston Marathon, shall forever remain seared in our national memory. Thus, have we arrived at perhaps the most crucial juncture of this document; the delineation of precisely what strategic frame of reference contains the greatest potential to mitigate these horrendous aspects of contemporary American society.

Beyond the matter of strategic considerations, what agenda of multi-faceted activities may, we as the citizens of the U.S., undertake to compel the miniscule population of those who control the financial/corporate destiny of our culture, to alter their course and proceed to an economic destination that shall bring into being an infinitely more egalitarian division of wealth.

For the course, I advocate will produce as well the corresponding reclamation by the overwhelming majority of our citizens of their political capacities to impact and influence the institutions that provide the structural frame of reference within which we exist. This endeavor also determines the content of those policies, programs, and activities responsible for defining the dynamics and the qualities operative in our daily lives.

It is my intent to fully delineate both the paradigm that, in my view, shall rectify the injustices of our contemporary structure of social arrangements, as well as the prospective and enormously salutary results, which the adoption of these institutions and processes will stimulate in chapters three and four.

CHAPTER THREE

*Creating and Implementing the Moral and Economic
Foundations of an American Future That is Equitable*

I t is my contention our contemporary social reality is pathological and
unjust with regard to the emaciated spiritual and material circumstances
in which many of our country are imprisoned. The question, obviously, becomes what alternative normative predicate and institutional construct contains the potential to rectify these injustices, and create an infinitely fuller
and more rewarding existence for our citizens in all areas of their lives?

I return to those values I cited in an earlier portion of this monograph,
i.e. the central concepts of the numerous religious traditions that are extant.
The similarities of these theological systems are remarkable, and the frequently minor and peripheral disagreements between them do not preclude
their unanimous advocacy of the intrinsic value of mankind. In addition, there
is a substantial consensus the source of their inherent liberty is derived from
a beneficent deity, and the obligations of the primary social contract and the
corresponding political processes which govern our lives (certainly in a West-
ern Democratic context) must allow and provide for the expression of these
freedoms. Moreover, also required as their birthright is the provision of the
basic human necessities by these sovereignties, that the opportunity to express

their individual persona, and their creative muse, as well as their potential by dint of conscientious and continuing individual exertion to create lives of material comfort, and demonstrate to their fellows the accomplishments their efforts have created.

I should hasten to add the fundamental values of a Humanist and existential philosophy cited previously, though not deriving validity from a transcendental deity, but rather places the originating location of these sentiments within the human community, supports and advocates the preceding religious systems contend is the requisite social environment. Is this some utopian vision, some extraordinarily fantasy that bears no possible relation to the attainment of contemporary social reality? I think not.

Many of the elements to which I refer already exist, and those that do not are certainly in a posture of pragmatic action and focused effort, lie within the realm of a possible American future. However, prior to the specific consideration of these manifold social experiments and models of economic democracy it is of critical importance to attribute these components of an emerging American culture to those particular stimulants and factors provoking this escalating surge of individual and collective institutional innovation.

It is beyond all else the transformational activism and intensifying desires of increasing segments of our society who wish to resuscitate their moribund souls, resurrect their consciousness, and rejuvenate a vigorous national morality. As important as it is to proclaim as their central credo, the concept that America's future must reflect the fundamental realities of a society in which ethical considerations, equitable cultural institutions, and self-transcendence, will ultimately prevail.

These goals shall be obtained.as the result of a dynamic and unceasing commitment of a growing constituency to the realization of this transformational ethos, which shall eventually witness the triumph of their efforts. The potential to glimpse and grasp the fundamental inquiry which must be addressed if we wish our lives to be purposeful and contain social value is as follows: "What precisely is the purpose of our existence?"

The requisite response is our lives must manifest in some unceasing behavioral regard, the allocation of our talents and abilities in the service of improving the collective social and cultural circumstances, in which we reside, that mitigate the burdens of the dispossessed among us.

The second responsibility we must assume is to construct those institutions and deploy the concomitant activism to attain the implementation of these models, in order to amplify the quotient of social justice our macrocosmic economic and political modalities embody and emit. In addition, there exists a companionate requirement to translate our fullest individual potential into actions and activities reflect a life whose muse and gifts are manifest in the joy, Eros, passion, artistic creativity, and humor with which we conduct our daily rounds and rituals. Thus, it is in this context of the complete expenditure of all that is our genetic legacy and we have acquired from our immersion in and exposure to sources of ethical nourishment we are asked to bequeath as our total contribution to our civilization and our individual evolution.

We have completed a major portion of our journey through the perplexing labyrinth we are required to navigate in order to remove the ideological cataracts and peel away normative delusions in which we have been ensnared. We finally enter the inner sanctum of the single most compelling responsibility, the quest for self-transcendence.

In this frame of reference, precisely what is it that constitutes the definition of "self-transcendence?" It is the attempt to explore as fully as is feasible the objective social reality of our lives with particular regard to the nature, content, and sources of the discontent, unhappiness, and lack of fulfillment present in our diurnal schedules.

The second element of this activity is the cognitive construction of a prospective alternative existence which would fully liberate and empirically actualize our talents, aptitudes, and passionate, creative impulses. In addition to these efforts, a crucial companionate endeavor to isolate and identify those cognitive and behavioral patterns we manifest, that are responsible for the harm we inflict upon our fellow citizens, in our daily interactions with them is an imperative task. It is through this examination of that which is absent in our existence that causes us great unhappiness and the unleashing of our muse, capacities, and fervor, as well as those deficiencies of character and ethical deportment that provokes irritation and, among others, we may embark upon a professional engagement and a personal trajectory that will sustain us. Moreover, it is these requisite spiritual and psychological exertions which will liberate us from our imprisonments and achieve a life of meaning, purpose, and an impact on those with whom we interact that is salutary and uplifting.

Subsequent to the completion of this process it becomes possible and imperative we begin the effort to transform our lives and our action, to conform to the ethical standards previously cited in the initial portion of this commentary.

The final task is to create those social, economic, political, and esthetic involvements that will stimulate the fullest possible actualization of one's capabilities and fervor, and by so doing significantly augment our sense of self-worth, joy, contentment, and personal tranquility.

The Pragmatic and Practical Dimensions
of Implementing the Previous Vision

As you review this document, many among you will determine the sentiments and prescriptions contained in my presentation, though laudable and relevant to our quest to create a more equitable society and humane cultural framework, do not address the matters central to a secular existence in this the twenty-first century of the American experience. In this presumption, you would be correct. However, it is my intent to commence the formulation of this agenda for a personal and social renaissance in very comprehensive and specific terms in this portion of my essay.

Perhaps the most critical of considerations regarding this mammoth task of humanizing our civilization we must address is the individual who wishes to commit to this laudable effort and how they might attain and retain in the longer term, the preservation of their families economic viability. To withdraw from various involvements in transnational corporate behemoths to reclaim the potential of participating in a lived experience that is multi-dimensional and self-actualizing is a crucial first step, but this act does not relieve us of our financial responsibilities to our families.

What are possible destinations for these courageous and noble pioneers that shall provide the requisite stream of revenue, as well as the organizational structures that are humane, innately equitable, an opportunity to acquire equity positions, profit sharing, and a sufficient retirement fund in which a maximally democratic system of administration is extant?

Armed with the results of your self-transcendence inventory becomes possible to chart a course of social entrepreneurialism where you are the master of your economic aspirations. The mission statement and strategic plan you formulate will reflect the fullest possible flowering of your normative system, and the muse you wish to allow the greatest possible empirical expression. Recently, increasing numbers of incubators in which technical and financial assistance is accessible to those who wish to create various enterprises in the realm of technology, biomedical, software, and most recently in New York, an incubator to stimulate the pursuit of artistic activity, gallery exhibits, and a commercial viability to support these artists in the longer term, have become effective functioning entities.

These repositories of expertise and monetary resources that can assist individuals in the establishment of commercial and non-profit ventures have

been created beneath the banner of state governments and municipal jurisdictions, as well as under the aegis of private innovators.

For those who are predisposed to contribute their intellectual, artistic,
financial, or political skills, to thousands of existing for-profit, not-for-profit,
non-profit organizations, and public-private partnerships addressing any aspect of those efforts required to create a humanistic multi-dimensional society, your computer will provide a roadmap for your journey, and an eventual
gateway to your professional future.

As your DBA (doing business as) evolves in terms of both revenue and
profitability, you may wish to avail yourself of the Benefit Corporation
Statutes that exist in a number of states, that permit corporations to consider
a matrix of concerns in their operations beyond the exclusive matter of max-
imizing profitability.

Such factors as levels of compensation to employees which permit them
to attain a robust middleclass status and beyond, to environmental considerations mitigate negative impacts, to the provision of affordable housing
for those in your employ who may require it, and a general continuing interest in the larger communities you are located, in terms of their challenges
and welfare, are among those relevant considerations. By availing yourself
of the protections, these statutes afford you are insulated from the legal obligation of many corporations who must maximize their profits, lest they
provoke litigation from disgruntled investors.

In Brooklyn, N.Y., and in other urban areas, a substantial proliferation in
the artisanal activities of specialty food produce and beverages, alcoholic and
non-alcoholic, has been occurring. For-profit, nonprofit, and not-for-profit, as
well as community economic development organizations, are allocating billions of dollar annually to public-private partnerships to rehabilitate distressed
neighborhoods and create employee owned and managed companies. These
entities provide products and services and occupational training programs,

which equip the unemployed with the requisite skills to obtain jobs that may culminate in a lengthy and remunerative career trajectory within the realm of organizations previously cited. Moreover, those individuals who are dedicated to the reform of both corporate and political macro-institutions, who advocate broadening the representation of employees, citizens, and unions on the boards of these transnational entities, would welcome additions to their ranks.

What primarily animates these efforts is the goal of attaining greater equitability in the relationship between the compensation levels of senior executives, and their infinitely more numerous subordinates. In addition, their agendas are concerned with the diminution of those corporate entities which impact the environment negatively, and are committed to broad and continuing support and assistance of and involvement with the communities in which they are situated. Moreover, there is an unceasing effort to insure employees have access at a very negligible financial cost to equity ownership in these organizations, in the form of stock options.

Beyond the previous initiatives is the crucial matter of democratizing hierarchical chains of administrative command, so employees may exert greater influence over the operations of the production processes and service obligations they are expected to discharge.

In the final analysis, so much of the alienation and estrangement these individual employees experience in the daily performance of their duties, is the fundamental sense of the dehumanization they experience, and the lack of dominion over their current assignments and their future career trajectories.

An additional aspect of their current discontent is the distribution of the increases in productivity these employees achieve in concert with technological innovations allocated disproportionately to senior management. Broader dimensions of political economic and social innovation can be found on such websites as "Basic Principles for a New Direction," which posits the essential specific actions required to create an equitable and sustainable economy.

Community Wealth.org presents the crucial forces which are gathering ever-greater momentum within local communities as the result of numerous public initiatives at the municipal and state echelons of government, and in unprecedented relationships between anchor institutions and local community based organizations, such as hospital and other healthcare facilities.

In these companies, equity ownership by their employees is substantial, and their impact and influence in administrative and operational spheres of its management are significant and continuing. In addition, various organizations, programs, and policies, which link in a bi-lateral posture university and community institutions, are stimulating the creation of community wealth and the increased abilities of citizens within these areas to obtain responsiveness from local governments previously nonexistent. Moreover, beneath the umbrella of the New Economy such entities as the Institute For Policy Studies, Economic Policy Institute, The New Economy Working Group, and the Levy Institute at Bard College are formulating new paradigms of economic development that are local attempts to provide alternatives to those models and entities which operate as traditional hierarchical systems.

It is these traditional structures that reflect enormous inequalities in the wealth and power among those who reside at the apogee of these organizations, i.e. the 1%, and the financial and political capacities of those who comprise the remaining 99%.

. In the realm of intellectual activity, which seeks to supplement and supplant traditional structures of public and corporate governance, such groups as the Alliance for Democracy, Center for Corporate Policy, Demos, and the Center for Digital Democracy, are vigorously engaged in the conceptual creation of new mechanisms, systems, and standards of measurement and evaluation. When implemented, these entities will remediate the grievous inequities and oppressive character of much that comprises the current

American social reality. In addition, these organizations will continue the rigorous critical analysis of existing institutions that are the ideological impediments obstruct our progress to a more egalitarian distribution of wealth, and the actualization of a vibrant multi-dimensional civilization.

One additional component of research, i.e. the techniques to successfully organize impoverished communities and to transform our national consciousness, are such entities as META, Political Economy of the Good Society, Center for Community Change, and Center for Third World Organizing.

The preceding enumeration is in no manner exhaustive or encyclopedic. However, it does reflect the breadth and depth of the spectrum of effort that is extant in our country. As increasing numbers of our citizens engage in the process of ethical inquiry, institutional evaluation, and exercises in self-transcendence their intense unhappiness with their personal circumstances and our cultures widening estrangement from those values will be revealed.

Those liberating concepts, which reside at the center of the theologies and the normative implications of the systems of philosophy previously cited, will provoke an escalation in the flow of those individuals who become refugees from rampant materialism and the parched soil on which competitive relationships, contrived scarcity, and social contentiousness, reign supreme.

If you are reading this document and are among those who thirst for a life in which cooperation, collaboration, and the individual flowering of your innate gifts and artistic proclivities can attain their maximum actualization, in the service of both the collective welfare of your fellow citizens and the fullest possible expression of a multidimensional personal existence, search no further.

A life composed of joy, passion, Eros, and specific projects and activities that call upon the talents, aptitude, and artistic and intellectual resources which you have been bequeathed and a rich network of sustainable and abundant friendships await you, as you commence your engagement with the labors many other citizens are already participating.

It is my perspective the most satisfying lives are experienced by those who attempt to navigate the tributary of self-transcendence, and subsequent to this process to either join with other individuals or organizations, or by the establishment of an entity that reflects your aspirations and embodies your goals for the exalted purpose of maintaining a continuity and consistent thread of behavioral fidelity to the moral principles you have formulated. Moreover, by placing your services in support of some effort among the millions of Americans who are currently engaged in the mammoth and unceasing exertions that will require decades to fully actualize, i.e. a homeland in which a vibrant Humanism is extant in every facet of our culture, will you experience an unprecedented sense of personal accomplishment.

What is so marvelous and sublime about this proposal is you will derive your financial viability from commitments to yourself and your loved ones consonant with and dynamically propel forward the evolution of our society toward sustainable, equitable, spiritual, and enormously fulfilling multi-dimensional lives, within a social atmosphere that honors the mitigation of suffering and the construction of those institutions that maximize social justice, beyond all else. No longer will you be required, in the name of monetary sufficiency, to toil at mind-numbing tasks in cramped cubicles in multinational corporations, whose preeminent concerns are the maximization of profit and the unceasing expansion of its dominion in a commercial context and through a vast and proliferating network of lobbyists.

By your withdrawal from these entities, you will disengage from their continuous quest to ensure the macro-political institutions that dispense justice, disgorge legislation, and perform tasks of regulatory oversight, produce results beneficial to the retention of their dominant stature, and insatiable expansionary appetites whether domestic or global in scope. Though the preceding sources of activity may be consulted at the various websites I have referenced vary in some partial regard, the core principles that define and breathe a robust and rewarding life into these dynamics, share at their epicenter a common embrace of those principles that define an egalitarian economic and political topography. They also manifest a current reality that fulfills the necessities of an individual and collective national life that is in some intrinsic regard reflective of ethical considerations, equitable cultural institutions, and a capacity to attain a state of self-transcendence.

Core Principles of the Social and Economic Innovations
That Animate Our Current Social Landscape

Among the specific optimal initiatives to which I am referring, is "The Cleveland Project" in the Midwest, the "Mondragon Cooperative" in the Basque region of Spain, or the various efforts to create State Banks to stimulate community based economic development, in such locales as North Dakota. These ingenious approaches are responsible for the formulation of equitable procedures of commercial operations and administration, which various programs in some of our most prestigious universities are creating, beneath the umbrella of social entrepreneurialism and enlightened entrepreneurship. Moreover, a Benefit Corporation legal status, which mandates the recognition of responsibilities to both their employees and the communities they are situated, rather than the traditional corporate obligation to maximize profits for their shareholders, demands the inclusion of ethical standards the deliberation of their Boards of Directors are governed.

This universe of enlightened institutions is united by the central assumption this era of American social decay and political impotence which afflicts so many in our nation, those companies must accept unprecedented responsibilities.

The transcendent obligation is to actively contribute beyond the provision of their products and services, to the rehabilitation and rejuvenation of this nation's democratic institutions and the companionate obligation, to ensure the resuscitation of our middleclass and the diminishment of poverty.

These multi-tier objectives will be actualized by supporting community based and managed commercial enterprises provide employment opportunities for those who are unemployed and underemployed. By doing so, these institutions will in a defacto posture be providing the services and products necessary to enrich the environments in our urban ghettos and rural wastelands, and create vibrant self-sustaining communities, afford much of the options and opportunities, which are present in comfortable middleclass environments.

For those who would suggest the expanded responsibilities inherent in this new broader corporate mandate are the obligations of government, I would respond in two regards: Government, at all levels, is beholden to and restricted by the wishes of many Fortune 500 corporations, as the result of the extraordinary influence the capital they provide to mount campaigns for office and/or to withhold these funds from candidates, who resist their will and agendas. Moreover, as the result of the transfer from corporations to the middleclass of much of the current tax burdens that fuel government operations, and with particular additional concerns for national debt and deficit considerations, as well as trade imbalances the funds to initiate these activities are severely circumscribed. Thus, is government precluded from undertaking these initiatives and projects, due to the lack of financial resources and the opposition of elites, lest their implementation result in the diminution of the social control and political potency, which this miniscule class of plutocrats exert.

With regard to the second element reflective of moral considerations among other aspects of relevance, is the fact the inequality and impotence of which constitutes much of our contemporary social reality has been created by these behemoths, and therefore, it is incumbent on these organizations to mitigate these pernicious and baleful cultural circumstances. Moreover, the financial resources of these companies are enormous and they are the sole repository at the present moment, with the fiscal capabilities to redress these grievances and rectify the injustices that they have inflicted.

The principles of economic democracy to which I refer are the foundation for both the structure of institutional arrangements, and their operational policies and administrative standards ,which are as follows:

- The establishment and operations of all commercial enterprises should be based within and subject to the collective strategic/administrative will of the board of directors and the employees of this entity. The composition of the board will reflect the following percentages of representation; 51% percent employees, (15% from the executive ranks of the organization) 15% representing investors/shareholders, and 14% from the community at large in which this entity is located.

- All decisions of the board must be determined as the result of a majority consensus of the board of directors/employees expressed in an annual electoral framework, and subsequently ratified by a majority vote of all employees.

- The menu of products/services which this organization provides to its customers shall also be determined by the previously cited majority consensus, i.e. board members and majority employee ratification, on an annual basis.

- The content of the responsibilities which each employee discharges shall be determined by the Human Resources Department, as well as the compensation provided for these tasks, etc., as well as training programs to ensure as broadly as possible that these individuals will acquire new skills to advance to increasing levels of participation/ contributions to the organizations growth and profitability.

- Inherent in each compensation plan will the explicit commitment to a self-sustaining wage, a stock options/equity shares formula, and pro-motions/salary increments for performance/innovations for deserving employees be included. These policies and financial/operational/admin-istrative rules and regulations shall be submitted to the board of direc-tors/for annual ratification and subsequent employee endorsement.

- All financial matters, investment considerations, operating budgets, incurring debt, dividends, possible mergers and acquisitions, strate-gic partnerships etc., shall be subject to majority board ratification, and the subsequent approval of the majority of its employees.

- All profits of the corporation shall be allocated to the following con-stituencies in the schedule which appears below:
  60% - Board of Directors, Shareholders/Investors, Employees, Bonuses
  25% - Reinvestment, Training, Technology Infrastructure etc.
  15% - Community Development Investment Fund (Low interest loans)

- Various municipal, state, and or federal agencies representatives such as those from Commerce, Urban/Rural Planning, Treasury, IRS, HUD, EDA, private community development funds etc., may attend these monthly Board meetings in an exclusively advisory capacity to apprise Board Members of those financial, governmental/private sector and technical resources, to which this company has access which could support its strategic mission and tactical approaches to greater revenues and profitability.

- CEO compensation packages must not exceed a multiple that is twenty times the value of the company's average employee yearly income.

- The company's total operational/administrative foot print shall reflect and embody sustainable economic principles whose impact preserves and protects the environment in which they are situated.

- A fundamental requirement of all contractual relationships that the company assumes shall be with organizations that reflect and embody the previously enunciated core principles of economic democracy whether domestic or in a foreign locale.

- All resources which are allocated in support of lobbying activity to influence any body of government, i.e. local, state, federal, regulatory, international entities, or litigation this company initiates, must be vetted by both the Board of Directors and ratified by a majority of its employees to ensure that whatever decision or determination is being sought from these entities does not contravene the community's and nation's public interest, and/or dilutes or mitigates the principles that appear above.

- Any objectives which do not diminish inequality in some regard and/or reduce poverty among our citizens, whatever additional elements of commercial self-interest they contain, shall be judged to be illegitimate and impermissible to pursue on behalf of the company.

The preceding enumeration of the primary normative components of commercial enterprises is neither fully rendered nor entirely comprehensive. Others may suggest revisions, alternative prescriptions, and/or additional considerations and concerns should be included in both the raison d'etre and the functioning of these entities is entirely appropriate and justified.

This effort will never in some complete sense be concluded, nor should it be; rather it is an emerging body of scholarship that is an attempt to be responsive to our current deplorable political and economic circumstances, and provide substantive and particularistic suggestions to achieve a redress of these financial and social afflictions.

Beyond all else, what I wish to convey to those of us who are fortunate enough to enjoy the benefits of citizenship in this nation is a unique and infinitely more activist posture of participation is required, if we wish to create a life for ourselves and our families and friends contains at its center, an organic engagement with a structure of ethical precepts. In addition, a parallel commitment to the construction and implementation of equitable institutions is necessary to realize those talents, creative energies, and artistic capacities will allow you to evolve throughout your existence in a self-actualizing context, and enlarge those values that define a society in which the concept of social justice is preeminent.

In the final analysis, this is the personal responsibility of all us to transcend our limitations and those qualities and characteristics which limit our compassion and empathy for others, and restrict our development as sentient and loving human beings.

The Unbroken Continuum
between our Personal Ethics and Our Societal Obligations

Wherever each of us currently resides on the spectrum of ethical concerns, the overwhelming majority of our fellow citizens embrace either some formal or informal religious affiliation/involvement, or a commitment to spiritual or Humanistic/Existential values or democratic principles that undergird our country's founding. Their content demands we accord to our fellow human beings intrinsic respect and innate value and inherent in status as sentient beings, are we endowed with inalienable individual liberties, and a social context in which manifold freedoms are extant. In addition, as it relates to our cultural experience, this nation is dedicated to the proposition that educational literacy in all its forms and economic opportunity, shall be accessible to each of our citizens regardless of race, creed, religious, and (non-religious) status, and as a result of these realities we may pursue the attainment in our life a happiness is both robust and enduring.

If you share these beliefs about your existence and that of those within your circle of loving relationships, does this system of values operate within your familial environment etc. but extends no further than the physical limits of your home or your workplace?

Do you operate from the fundamental assumption beyond the sphere of your interpersonal relationships, little if anything of substance or significance can be achieved as it relates to the implementation of these moral considerations or ethical precepts, in the larger society? Furthermore, are you of the opinion powerful institutions and contemporary social arrangements don't function in an aggregate manner and produce a profoundly inimical, toxic, and inhumane, atmosphere in which we reside?

If you embrace these erroneous presumptions it is imperative you consider two possible courses of action. Should you continue your allegiance to these ideas and the impotence and inaction which they breed, this apathy and indolence, in concert with that of many other Americans, will presage our national decomposition. Your resignation to this posture of powerlessness and immobility shall ensure our nation will fail as an audacious experiment in democracy, and ultimately this grievous lack of success shall give rise to increasing instability and the disintegration of our commonweal, in a lengthy and agonizing process of discontinuity. Rather, should you adopt a course of action and superimpose your moral frame of reference upon the commercial enterprise in which you are employed, and other commercial enterprises in this category whose products or services you patronize. Moreover, if you determine, as the result of your analysis, Fortune 500 companies and private companies of equivalent revenues and profitability, function in a manner that advances the community's public interest, i.e. the rejuvenation of the vibrancy and influence of local public institutions, the strengthening of the local economy, and the mitigation of social blight and communal dysfunction, then these are entities worthy of your continued patronage.

Obviously, in the instances in which the scope of this organization's activities is regional, national, or transnational, applying these standards of evaluation in a larger geographical context is without question necessary. Moreover, this evaluation must include all environmental impacts their operations register, be it benign or malignant, and be responsive beyond that to the requirements which a model of sustainability demands, as the ultimate mode of the provision of products and services by this entity. However, beyond the previous concerns additional crucial standards of measurement must be implemented to determine whether the operating practices of these companies reflects both a vibrant code of ethics in interactions with consumers, the general public, employees, investors, shareholders, and supports the public interest within the entire realm of its global impact.

A Comprehensive Instrument to Evaluate All Activities of Fortune 500 Companies Internal Management/Compensation Practices/ Environmental Practices/External Relations

- Are employees compensated at levels that minimally permit the individual to be financially self-sustaining in the absence of any governmental programs of support and/or additional jobs? (A minimum wage of twenty dollars per hour)

- Do these positions provide integral to their entire packages adequate health coverage for both the individual and his family, to which both the employer and employee contribute in an equitable manner?

- Do these employers provide paid vacations for their employees?

- Is compensated sick leave also an element of their total wage package?

- Do any policies exist in any regard may be deemed discriminatory to the hiring, retention, and/or advancement, of any employee because of race, gender, sexual orientation, or religious affiliation?

- Are employees compensated for those hours beyond the normal work day at minimally time and a half or greater for their additional efforts?

- Are the workplaces in which they expend their energies, safe, clean, well- lighted, climate controlled, and comfortable and pleasant environments?

- Do supervisors treat their subordinates with respect, and humanely, as well as allowing these individuals the formal capacity to provide contributions to the formulation and implementation of work schedules, manufacturing processes, and administrative and operational/logistical aspects, of the production/service process?

- Are employee grievances adjudicated in an impartial manner/process that insures that irrespective of the specific result the complainant has been given the opportunity to be heard and responded to in an equitable procedure?

- Are employees represented on the Board of Directors as formal voting members?

- Do these companies allocate a portion of productivity increases as compensation to their employees, i.e. non senior executives of these organizations?

- Do these commercial enterprises provide compensated parental leave to their employees?

- Have these entities established and maintained appropriate supervised daycare facilities, and/or in their absence an employee stipend to obtain childcare for their children?

- Do these commercial enterprises utilize revenues/profits to purchase their company's shares of stock that are traded on public exchanges, in order to increase the price per share?

- Do these corporations provide substantial portions of their profits for reinvestment purposes in the company, to enable such activities as business expansion, employee training and development, and technological improvements in the various facets of the company's activities?

- Are dividend payments to shareholders modest as opposed to exorbitant?

- Do CEO's and other senior management personnel receive a ratio that is greater than 20 to 1 of the median wage of the company employee?

- Are financial debts incurred by the company to provide the funds to conduct any portion of the organization's activities?

- In the event of either declining profits or revenues on an annual basis are senior executives penalized for these declines/or removed?

- Do employees sit on all committees of the Board; put particularly those responsible for charting the strategic objectives the corporation wishes to pursue, in the immediate and longer term?

- Do these organizations provide grants/low interest loans to local/regional/national/international community economic development projects, specifically created to increase employment and mitigate various aspects of poverty? In their geographical regions of activity?

- Do these entities negatively impact the maintenance and perpetua tion of sustainable environments as the result of their manufacturing/operations processes?

- Have they integral to their multi-year strategic planning committed to the elimination of these activities as rapidly as is feasible?

- In the interim, do they provide the financial, technical, and administrative resources, required to neutralize the negative impacts of their current modus operandi?

- Do they engage in any formal contractual relationships with companies who are guilty of committing these or related injuries to our nation's or a global planetary sustainability?

- Do they support in terms of their public relations, marketing, and advertising campaigns, those policies whether NGO, governmental, or private sector in origin, which seek to diminish those commercial activities which contribute to global warming/climate change?

- As the result of contractual relationships with countries that possess substantial natural resources, do these companies support non-democratic governments and/or contribute to the financial disparity and political tyranny, in which almost all citizens of these totalitarian societies are mired?

- Do these companies provide loaned executives to organizations which seek to expand educational excellence and/or economic opportunity?

- Do the values which the corporations philanthropic foundation reflect, seek the improvement and efficacy of institutions that exist to

diminish social dysfunction, familial disintegration, and the augmented creation of effective educational organizations and employment opportunities?

- Finally, are these commercial enterprises in some total regard mani-
festing those ethical principles and a system of morality, which may be
glimpsed in the religious and philosophic formulations of virtually all
major theologies and within the Humanist and Existential traditions?

The preceding compilation of evaluative tools is not a complete enunciation
of every single legitimate requirement Fortune 500 companies and/or other
nonpublic behemoths should be subject. However, it is a point of departure
from these entities may be measured to determine whether or not they are
currently functioning in the public interest, according to standards infinitely
broader than those by which corporations have been historically evaluated.
Most importantly, they are contributing in their operations, actions, and public pronouncements, to the resurrection of a climate, which will enable our
citizens to reclaim their jurisdiction over those processes by which public decisions are reached, and the equitability of the formulas and procedures by
which wealth is distributed in America.

I have delineated in this chapter both those paradigms of economic
activity and organizational objectives comprise, in my view, the reality of
an emerging and enlarging alternative American society. Within that paradigm, the cumulative objectives of these entities happily conspire to both
resuscitate the potency of this nation's democratic institutions, and the reclamation thereby of a political process in which the majority of our citizens
shall determine our future and our fate. In addition, I have exposed the
multi-faceted efforts of various community based nonprofit, for profit, not-
for- profit entities to create and expand those local economic development

vehicles that operate in accordance with democratic management principles, compensation packages that contain stock options at a very modest cost and permit the attainment of a middleclass status. Also contained within this process of manufacture and/or service provision, are those operational requirements that supports a sustainable environment, contribute to the mitigation of poverty in their communities either directly or indirectly, and to those initiatives within these locales, that attempt to bolster the reinvigoration of the cultural climate and physical reconstitution of urban ghettos and rural wastelands, within their sphere of activities and political influence.

Beyond, I have provided a structure of evaluation by which Fortune 500 companies and their private counterparts in terms of revenue and profitability should be judged. However, in order to accomplish the previous objectives are the process and mechanisms, I am advocating, assisting these democratic and community based economic organizations to achieve a preponderant mass of commercial enterprises ultimately dwarf all other structures of commercial enterprises not dedicated to these principles. But, perhaps most importantly, a second objective I believe is crucially imperative is to implement those initiatives that will compel the plutocrats and the corporate behemoths which they sit astride, to reform their strategic objectives and cease the activities they currently fuel.

These actions perpetuate economic inequality, the continuing attrition of the influence of the majority of our populace to affect our political institutional decision-making and thus, our destiny as a nation. They are responsible, as well, for the continuing perpetuation of social decay, physical deterioration, and the enlargement of those citizens who have been consigned to the inhospitable basement of poverty in the United States.

CHAPTER FOUR

*A Prospective Course of Individual Action That Both Maximizes
Your Human Potential and Happiness and Liberates This
Nation from Our Collective Impotence and Impoverishment*

Among the more than 320 million Americans who currently reside in our nation, contemporary life, for all the reasons I have previously enumerated, is a challenging, complex, demanding, and most stressful exercise in negotiating the numerous demands to which we must be responsive.

Within our intimate interpersonal relationships, employment responsibilities, (and in the allocation of whatever energies remain unexpended) the various involvements civic and religious/spiritual in character, as well as rare attempts to engage in recreation, entertainment, and vacation periods or leisurely pursuits, require. Thus, the prospect of assuming yet additional burdens in the service of those individual engagements and societal obligations, however noble in their intrinsic character, would be greeted by almost all of us as beyond our present capacities; prospective exertions for which we possess neither the physical energy nor mental capacities. However, it is my respectful, and I would argue a reflection of an accurate objective social reality, the agenda of participation it is my fervent hope numerous citizens shall presently assume, lies within our grasp and our human capacities. All that is required to engage with these efforts is the quantitative reduction of those areas of participation within our lives, not its qualitative abandonment.

To examine the totality of your life, to determine a possible strategy to express those talents and capabilities your current career trajectory precludes, to formulate specific alterations in your behavior that elevates your capability to be loving, empathetic, and respectful in your dealings with others, are the most critical activities to which you may devote yourself. Moreover, if your wish is to experience a life of maximum personal joy and the simultaneous contribution to those citizens, who are committed to greatly increase the quotient of social justice that is operative, it is this journey on the path of self-transcendence and collective altruism that shall lead to this destination.

All major theologies request we unceasingly explore our conduct, motives, and frames of intellectual reference in order that we may achieve greater personal happiness and augmented contributions to the social environment in which we live, i.e. the welfare of the commonweal. For Jews, this process is contained in the High Holy Day of Yom Kippur. For those who are devout Catholics, the confessional serves this purpose of acknowledgement and ethical rededication. In other faiths throughout the world, there are opportunities and obligations to critically examine our conduct and recommit ourselves to the intensified behavioral implementation of our beliefs in our daily lives.

To those of you who upon reading the forgoing are dismissing these views as the absurd idealistic notions of the naïve or the unsophisticated, that reflect a scant understanding of the actual manner in which our society functions, I, respectfully, reject that assessment. If the reader has derived nothing else from the preceding elements of this document, it most assuredly should be the minimal comprehension I possess a substantial awareness of the fundamental realities of contemporary America. Moreover, it is precisely my acknowledgement of the "pragmatic realities of the status quo," its normative foundations, and its macro-institutional structures that must be dismantled and replaced with a rehabilitated system, that will release us from the inequities of realism, that is oppressive and dehumanizing.

Do the daily rituals and routines of your current existence and the organization you contribute your energies and expertise (in excess of fifty hours for many of us), provide beyond a material reward, which reflects financial stagnation, and a career advancement track that has been all but obstructed, and in which the prospect of a promotion looms far in your future, if at all? Do your daily commutes require you rise before dawn and return long after the sun's disappearance? Are stress anxiety and exhaustion common companions in your daily routines? Do you nibble at dinner, barely aware of its contents and find the conversations of your family members to be too challenging to interpret and respond to? Are the parental obligations of monitoring your children's homework and general academic progress, being in some important regard neglected by those distractions and anxieties that gnaw and your psyche, and inhabit your awareness? Are you embroiled in arguments with your spouse/partner on frequent occasion reflect various areas of your lives which so much that is dissatisfying and inadequate about their content and essence, is perpetually reiterated?

Finally, at the conclusion of this schedule of activities do you sink into the cushions of your couch semi-comatose, enervated, and devote the final hours before bed to the escapist fare of television programs that continually push forward the boundaries of sexual entanglements, and/or ever more gaudy and brutal violent scenarios of combat and crime?

Or do you turn to the online seductiveness of your computer's menu spam and email, to immerse yourself in a continuing bombardment of advertisements and video games that offer relationships, sexual stimulants, lines of credit, and a unending array of solicitations for virtually any product or service?

Do you, when your interest in the forgoing is satisfied, crawl over numerous websites out of boredom or a feigned anemic interest in these subjects presented in the time honored American tradition of killing time? Do weekends consist of a frenzied blur of soccer matches, ballet classes, playdates, birthday parties, and Saturday evenings with friends at a restaurant, film, drama, or orchestral production in which those in attendance chat about their child's exploits, an acquaintances misfortune or divorce, the problems at work, or impending vacations?

Should you conclude from my preceding comment I, in some posture of contempt or condescension, believe the subjects which are topics of conversation are not significant or deserve discussion, you would be in error. However, the point of the forgoing is rarely are there addressed in these social events matters lie outside the realm of our personal lives.

My wish is not that these interactions should not be continued in their present form, but rather in addition to the microcosmic components of our lives, we enlarge our dialogue to include considerations of a macro character as well. Much about the shape and ingredients of our individual circumstances are the result of those institutions and dynamics ascendant in this nation and it is in their transformation at a cultural level we shall experience infinitely greater choice and possibilities, and thus, a life in which self-transcendence and a robust and vibrant happiness is achievable.

If you have determined much of your life does not in any enduring or meaningful regard provide you with a sense of accomplishment, or furnish you with the opportunity to express your various creative talents and aptitudes, you are not alone. If it is fraught with insecurity, anxiety, and unremitting pressures that are the result of your current financial circumstances my agenda will provide the specific tools to release you from this dehumanizing and oppressive quality of life. If it is your wish to exit from these inimical influences, without jeopardizing your family's economic circumstance, and transition to a life which permits the fullest possible flowering of your ethical impulses, in the personal dimensions and the broader macrocosm of your professional and civic life, the instrumentality to achieve that is at your disposal. If you wish to join the exploding numbers of our citizens engaged in the campaign to simultaneously dismantle those forces in American life that continue to erode the efficacy of political institutions and increase the unprecedented levels of material inequality, they will welcome you with open arms.

It is these influences that ultimately imperil the planet's continuance as the result of global policies which are destroying our eco-systems, and the larger environmental framework in which seven billion souls are struggling to remain viable. This grand endeavor will provide an effective opportunity to transform your lives and the existences of all our countrymen, as well as the cultural organism, in which we all coexist.

It is my hope the matters I am addressing are of importance to your life, and to a companionate desire to become if you have not already commenced these efforts, a party to these noble and imperative collective exertions. However, there may be among you those who believe the intellectual energy and time frames required to undertake these involvements are substantial, demanding, and lie beyond the possibility of your schedule and logistics.

The happy news is that is not at all the reality. In this the penultimate chapter of this document I shall delineate the actual mechanisms and processes I intend to create in the very near future to accomplish our objectives and continue the reclamation of America.

CHAPTER FIVE

*Two Standards of Moral Measurement to both Define Exemplary
Commercial Enterprises and Identify Those Corporate Culprits
Whose Manifold Realties Are Among the Most Reprehensible*

I n the recent past, as my concerns for this nation's future intensified, I
thought to add to the dialogue occurring in an analytic and prescriptive
aspect of scholarship, might hopefully enrich the conversation and provide
various perspectives that may not have been either included or sufficiently
emphasized. Thus, in 2013 I reactivated the website I had created a number
of years ago that had been neglected as the result of more pressing project
involvements, i.e. "The Center for Humanistic Initiatives." The address for
this activity is chgi.WordPress.Com. Central elements of this manuscript
were preliminarily developed in a much more abbreviated document
"America's Future: Requiem or Transformation?" which appears on this
website. However, crucially absent among other important components of
this text were specific standards of evaluation by which the citizens of this
nation might be capable of furthering the expansion of those commercial
enterprises, that reflect and embody those strategic objectives.

They also embrace those entities whose operating principles provide adequate salaries and equity positions in these organizations, as well as augment the influence employees wield regarding management goals and administrative procedures.

For it is my considered judgment one critical element of the strategy to mitigate inequality and resurrect the political efficacy of the majority of our citizens, is to support the creation of ever-greater numbers of community-based economic development vehicles. Moreover, those entities demonstrated a fidelity to democratic management processes and furnish compensation packages enable their employees to achieve and retain a middleclass status, should be rewarded by an ever-ascending stream of consumer revenue. Thus, through the efforts of our financial support for these commercial operations we will witness the growth of their scope and impact from local communities, to regional, and ultimately national, and international, institutions. Though this goal is one that will require years of effort, ultimately we will, as the result of these exertions, witness the advent of a "critical mass," and beyond that not long thereafter, a majoritarian presence of these forms of commerce on the cultural landscape of this nation.

When that objective is realized, much of what I am advocating regarding the moral and political rejuvenation of the United States will have been attained.

To those of you who are involved with a whole host of activities that are attempts to democratize our society, and mitigate those variables comprise the landscape of a disintegrating commonweal, I commend you to a vigorous and uninterrupted continuation of these involvements.

In my view, it is not simply and solely one track or approach to the result of a moral and just society, but rather, a whole host of simultaneous efforts involve the electoral process, demonstrations of citizen outrage, and financial contributions to enlightened candidates. These efforts should also be supplemented by litigation to redress grievous actions of corporate mis-creants, advocacy for international overtures to stem climate warming, and replace the avarice of unrestrained consumption with the policies which sup-port a global economic reality, that reflects a sustainable ethic. However, I should like to include one additional activity available to all citizens with minimal investitures of time and energy, and that brings me to the second and, perhaps most crucial, prospective activity I am advocating.

In my view, above all other activities this initiative contains the potential, in a relatively brief period of time, to provide the requisite impact on mam-moth corporate entities public and private, to cease practices morally be-nighted, accelerate inequality, and erode the efficacy of political institutions, as well as desecrate our environment. The stark choice which awaits them is to either reform their modus operandi or face financial extinction.

It is my intent when this manuscript has been completed and submitted to an appropriate publishing company for dissemination to the citizens of this nation and other interested international constituencies, to create at the heart of my website, i.e. chgi.wordpress.com, two continuing inventories of commercial enterprise activity in the U.S.

The first compilation shall be entitled "Ethical Commerce," which will continue to explore and highlight those companies domestically and overseas reflect in their ethos, operations, and public pronouncements, and supporting initiatives, those principles inherent in community based economic develop-ment enterprises.

I remain fervently committed to these activities beyond all other para-digms because given their principle of democratic decision making and the entire spectrum of associated values and ideals they embody, the impact on all aspects of the communities they serve and are situated, in will derive the greatest benefits from their presence. I shall, on a monthly basis, include status reports of all significant developments about these enterprises. Their successes and the specifics of those challenges or difficulties they are confronting, the areas of the nation they operate, as well as the addresses and phone numbers of their companies' headquarters.

Beyond the previous profile, revenues and profitability will be cited and other factors to ensure these companies remain in compliance with those standards necessary to be classified as a part of the universe of "Ethical Commerce."

It is my hope you and all of our citizens would support these entities by your continuing patronage, to stimulate the expansion of their current operational arc, to become a regional presence, and ultimately a national and international economic factor of significant salutary influence.

The second continuing evaluative exercise will present the central and defining realities of those Fortune 500 public companies and major private corporations, as well as those that comprise an inventory of private hedge funds and related financial institutions. At the heart of this compendium, data will appear that relates to their conformity to or deviance from those principles that define exemplary conduct in the quality of their products and services, and equally important as moral actors either contribute to or detract from, our nation's public interest and welfare. That these anticipated efforts are not revolutionary or precedent establishing in their prospective functioning is without question an undeniable fact. Rather, I am happily guilty of an act of intellectual plagiarism in the adoption of these mechanisms.

For decades, the publication "Consumer Reports" has provided, in my view, an invaluable service to the American consumer, in which without prejudice or bias in any form, it has acquired and subjected to rigorous performance standards, virtually the entire spectrum of products available to the public for purchase. Though they have occasionally been subjected to attempts to cajole and accept material inducements, or have been subjected to threats of litigation, they have remained an impartial arbiter committed exclusively to but one goal, the impartial objective assessment of a product or service. Their exclusive mission is to compare items within an identical or similar category of operation, and ultimately to determine in precisely what ranking these may be classified, from the best value, to that product which has, in the estimation of those technical experts the least worth. That they have succeeded in this continuing service is without question, and virtually never has there arisen a controversy regarding their methods or fairness of the processes employed in reaching their conclusions.

They remain, to this day, a beacon of integrity and continuing relevance to the consumer. When their advice has been heeded from a financial standpoint and with regard to the time consuming and often frustrating efforts required to replace defective merchandise, and other aspects of unsatisfactory operation, have they been enormously helpful.

More recently, in the realm of nonprofits there has been created an entity that provides, in my view, an invaluable service to those who operate nonprofit organizations, and most importantly to that community of prospective donors who are extending serious consideration to contributing funds, to enable a particular organization to discharge its service mandate. This organization, i.e. Charity Navigator, evaluates the entire spectrum of activity in which specific nonprofits are engaged, their expenditures, their fund raising procedures, their operation and programmatic initiatives, and virtually every other facet of their organizational reality.

Subsequent to this review, they provide a grade A-F that reflects in a cumulative regard, the degree to which this agency is efficient, competent, and cost-effective, in the manner in which it generates funds, and in the quality of services they provide to their client constituency. Frequently, though those groups that receive mediocre or deficient grades may be irritated by this finding, often utilize the specific criticisms to improve their practices and operations and achieve improved grades in future evaluations as the result of these modifications. Thus, this process has contributed greatly to prospective donors who by consulting an objective and balanced estimate of that entity become apprised of the concerns, which Charity Navigator has unearthed. Moreover, these evaluative mechanisms have assisted consumers and those with philanthropic predispositions to acquire products or access services excellent and worthy of their prices manufacturers or service providers have affixed to them. It also aids them in identifying those organizations that serve their client constituencies with programmatic competence in a cost-efficient manner.

It is my intention to deploy these standards of measurement in the infinitely more important task of expanding the national realm of community economic development activities, and all that flows from the augmentation of that presence and operational dynamic in our society.

In addition, this assessment tool will aid our personal quest to attain a life of self-actualization, and the companionate contribution of our skills and talents, in the service of incrementally elevating the quotient of social justice that is extant in our commonweal.

Among the thousands of audacious experiments unfolding within this marvelous world of "Ethical Commerce," may well be an entity that could provide for your exit from a life of boredom, anxiety, a soul-deadening career agenda, and schedule of obligations to a professional involvement infinitely more rewarding in every sense of the term.

This indispensable compilation of commercial enterprises will provide the dual possibilities of enabling our citizenry to act as discriminating consumers and, by doing so, meaningfully contribute to the transformation of America, and discover the existence of organizations which might become a destination for the their talents or energies. Moreover, though this compendium may inspire us to create those businesses or non-profit/not-for-profit/for-profit models, previously enumerated in a posture of enlightened social entrepreneurialism, it pales before the potential efficacy of the second and most important use which the analytic instrumentality, i.e.

"Commercial Reprobates," will furnish. It is in this enumeration I shall, in all its reprehensible grandeur, display a portrait of those public and private companies responsible for so much that contributes to the unraveling of our middleclass, and the misery of those who dwell in poverty in this nation, and well as the coarsening of our moral sensibilities and intellectual deterioration.

These are the institutional culprits who are responsible for so much amiss in the U.S. at this moment. Their exclusive concerns in the instance of those with a public status relate to share price, revenues, and profitability, and stratospheric compensation packages, dividends, and ensuring so much of their assets remain outside the jurisdiction of our I.R.S. Thus, it is in the vocabulary of interdicting the flow of consumer revenues that we must address these entities to gain their attention, and ultimately compel them to rectify their immoral behaviors and repair the enormous damage for which they are primarily responsible.

We, as citizens, must deploy, as a disciplining weapon, the terminology of rejection of their modus operandi as commercial enterprises. We must as a nation of more than 320 million consumers convey the following message to these rampaging behemoths, who seek continued mercantile and political hegemony.

You're continuing capacity to reside in palatial fortresses and obscene material luxury and enjoy lives of extraordinary indulgence, at the grievous expense of so many of your fellow citizens and others throughout the globe, is in grave jeopardy.

The era of calloused indifference to the plight and welfare of those who are not a party to your tables of organization, your pools of investors and shareholders, and those in our political class at all levels who do your bidding and ensure the perpetuation of the deplorable national status quo over which you have presided, will be brought to an abrupt and complete termination.

We shall achieve those objectives as a unified group of consumers by withholding the one commodity which enables your corporate existence and all that derives from that reality; those dollars that have historically been provided to you in the form of purchases for your products and services.

Should your company prohibit employees from membership on the board of directors, this fact will be duly noted and publicized. Should you provide compensation levels beneath twenty dollars an hour to those in your employ, we shall provide that information to the consuming public. Should your employees be denied the opportunity to acquire as the result of their faithful and diligent labor, equity positions in your corporation on terms affordable for the average wage earner, that negative circumstance will be an element to be considered in our evaluation.

Should you engage in arbitrary decisions regarding operational aspects of your company's presence in a community or locale, and depart from these facilities without either informing those affected or permitting a possible transition to employee management/ownership these facts will be disseminated about your enterprise's business practices.

Should those companies with whom you are engaged in contractual relationships reflect any element of the previously enumerated table of activities, that reality will be made known to the public.

Should your manufacturing/service/distributional procedures negatively impact on the environment in which your operations are situated and/or anywhere on the globe that is ecologically damaged as a result, will these baleful processes become part of the public record.

Should the policies and actions which your company embraces and supports hamper and obstruct the creation of a sustainable economy, both domestically within the U.S. or elsewhere on the globe, rest assured this knowledge will be shared with the citizens of this nation.

Should your company be guilty of excluding racial or religious minorities or individuals whatever their gender or sexual predispositions, these prejudices shall be cited on our blog updates, as they come to our attention.

Should the lobbyists, consultants, or the legal expertise whom you have retained, seek legislative, regulatory, or judicial objectives that benefit your company, but do so at the further expense of those factors previously cited, i.e. to the detriment of our public interest, will these actions appear in a prominent locale on our website.

Should you remain aloof from the communities in which you are situated with regard to assisting various other private and public actors in addressing in some manner the dysfunction, poverty, blight, and lack of educational and training programs, this detachment won't remain hidden.

Should you remain indifferent to creating employment opportunities for those currently unemployed or other challenges to the welfare and well-being of these residents, this civic aloofness will become part of your company's profile and be featured on our periodic updates.

If contributions from your PAC support those who are incumbents or others seeking political office that wish to maintain the current ascendant value system and the social arrangements which undergird it, these financial transactions shall find their way to our honor roll where all our readers may review this material.

In regard to those private companies such as hedge funds, and other monetary entities, which have placed under their management hundreds of billions of dollars, the most important information I shall attempt to obtain about these financial institutions is:

- Total resources under management
- Investments into which these sums are inserted
- The return on these investments

- The list of those individuals and organizations who have provided these funds
- The compensation provided to fund managers i.e. fees, commissions, bonuses, salaries, etc.
- The impact these investments register on the such indices of measurement as job creation, mitigation of poverty within the geographic area within which these sums are deployed, etc,
- What percentage of these investments are involved in arcane financial transactions such as arbitrage, credit default swaps, insurance or reinsurance programs, equity and bond purchases, loans to banks or companies (for what purpose), and related activities?
- PAC's that represent their political agendas; and what specific political, economic objectives/candidates,(they wish to accomplish and support for electoral office)
- Investments in foreign companies or governments? For what purposes?
- Beyond all else is the matter of transparency, i.e. the full release of responses to these questions and any additional data regarding any aspect of their operations/activities

Should you engage in arcane and complex transactions in the world of miniscule differentials between the trading values of respective sovereign currencies, credit derivatives, arbitrage, and "dark pools," and electronically "delayed" transactions, the citizens of this nation shall be made abundantly aware.

Should you assume excessive risk positions in highly leveraged investments, and are among the very few U.S. entities comprise the "too big to fail" segment of our economy, we shall continuously expose your practices and activities to our populace. In addition, we shall vigorously recommend to those citizens who are patronizing "Ethical Commercial" enterprises the cessation of all purchases from companies that find their way to our list of "Commercial Reprobates."

Should they be among the millions of Americans who are members of pension funds, to demand these fund managers suspend all relations with these investment vehicles and find other channels and opportunities, which stimulate the development of community, based economic vehicles and all the beneficial realities they presuppose.

Though these funds occasionally provide slightly better returns on the sums invested than traditional IPO's or more risk averse private placements, they serve no purpose relevant to infrastructure improvement, business creation, employment opportunities, and civic improvement projects.

They circulate within the previously articulated world of investments that benefit those who are enormously wealthy, but have virtually no impact on the world in which the overwhelming majority of our citizens function and reside. However, the single most devastating fact about these investment funds is, by virtue of the fact they commit the trillions of dollars they manage to these esoteric and ephemeral transactions, ensures these vast sums are not available to the this nation for such beneficial purposes cited above, which would significantly mitigate inequality and reinvigorate the influence which the majority of our citizens yield in the process of political decision-making,

It is almost impossible to conceptualize the extraordinary impact the appropriate use of these funds might achieve were they allocated to socially beneficial purposes. Suffice it to state these trillions of dollars would enormously enrich our cultural atmosphere and our material circumstances as a population, and substantially reduce the friction and contentiousness which is extant at this moment in the life of our society.

The Creation and Maintenance of the "Ethical Commerce"
and "Commercial Reprobates" Standards of Evaluation

It is my intent, immediately upon completing this manuscript and the attendant tasks of its editing, to submit it to the appropriate publisher. My hope is it will be received by the American public as a worthy addition to our current national dialogue about our challenges and prospective solutions. However, whatever its fate in that regard, it is my intent to address the formulation and continuing maintenance of the previously cited categories of assessment, in order that we might patronize these entities and contribute to their growth and expansion into regional, national, and international institutions that will ultimately dominate our social landscape in a posture of "critical mass."

Simultaneously, by publicizing the activities of those companies which comprise the "Commercial Reprobates" compilation, will spur the gradual discontinuance of the purchases by the general consuming public of their products and services.

The unrelenting glare of exposure will either compel the normative and structural reform of those companies or, through financial insolvency, cause the extinction of these entities that currently wield such wealth and influence, in the service of their benighted morality and oppressive economic and political agendas.

What is required then of the consuming public? To cease the use of the Internet or decline trips to TJ Maxx or Macy's? Abandon your role as responsible parents and partners? Dispense with your friendships and vacations or support for various college or professional athletic franchises? Discard your periods of evening relaxation enmeshed in various films or television series? In any substantive regard alter your current life as it is structured? Not at all. What I am requesting of all of our citizens who find our contemporary financial and political situation as a republic reprehensible is to diminish the energies and the time allotted to the previous activities, and instead devote one hour per week to a ceaseless examination of the status and progress which the preceding twin campaigns are attaining.

It is in the dynamic commitment to these goals by all our citizens that will support the viability and expansion of companies who are engaged in the practices of commerce that are ethical, and whenever and wherever feasible to totally cease any and all financial transactions with those whose modus operandi is to continue the current deplorable social realities ad nauseam ad infinitum.

What I am attempting to create is the commencement of a national tradition which has annual acknowledgements, and weekly elements. Throughout our history, we have celebrated holidays to commemorate civic leaders and their influence on our evolution as a people, such as Lincoln, Washington, and Dr. King. Moreover, we provide annual acknowledgments of the fathers and mothers among us without whom our maturity and moral sensibilities would be anemic. In addition, there exist other festivals of countless number at every level of our culture, i.e. local, state, and regional celebrations, as well as those in which the entirety of our nation pays tribute in an annual act of recognition. Surely, to inaugurate at this critical moment of our national life a formal declaration which requests we inquire as a people whether we are diminishing those facets of our culture that reflect great inequity and social dysfunction, and augmenting the quotient of both personal and collective fulfillment and well-being on an annual basis, is legitimate, justified, and imperative.

Let us determine, from this point forward, on the afternoon of the first Saturday of October of each year, we shall engage in a national process of civic evaluation and personal assessment. Examine in considerable detail and comprehensiveness the two most significant portions of our life and our consciousness, e.g. the civic and the individual.

Part one of this inventory will be allocated to an analysis of the progress or retrenchment we attained in the previous twelve month period regarding matters of poverty, inequality, employee participation in the governance of the companies in which they are employed, etc.

In addition, we shall evaluate environmental impacts (positive and negative), the national and international conduct of major corporations and private entities, and, most importantly, the impact which the majority of our citizens are registering on our policy formulation and the political decisions we have adopted as a commonweal. Moreover, beyond the matter of supporting ethical commerce and the cessation of any commercial activities with those firms appear on a commercial reprobates list. What other possible involvements might you consider in a model of voluntary service to various community entities that exist to mitigate poverty, or various aspects of social dysfunction?

Beyond the previous areas of consideration to commit your energies to improve educational and/or job training programs, and expand the participation by those who are high school graduates and receiving the minimum wage for their labors, to join the ranks of the married and reap the economic advancement for their families, which this status presupposes.

The second element will consist of a comprehensive inquiry into the lives of you and your family members in three particular respects. Are you deriving from your career involvement the opportunity from a compensation package and work environment standpoint, the ability to attain and retain a middleclass existence?

Do you experience a sense of personal satisfaction regarding your capability to influence the management practices extant in your organization, as well as the ability to express your talents and energies within this occupational context?

Finally, in terms of the family dynamics, are there areas in which all parties might improve their actions to reflect a more loving and considerate mode of behavior? What specific modifications are required to achieve those improvements in the quality of life and the happiness quotient that exists in your daily interactions?

To contend the average American family would not devote a day to this effort, I would suggest otherwise. Subtracting one day in the lives of individuals from an annual schedule of other concerns and priorities that will provide enormous benefits to themselves and their communities is surely an exercise in self-interest and in the public welfare of this society.

It is my fervent belief this dual economic strategy of financial reward and penalization, when combined with those efforts that reflect democratizing aspirations that originate in labor unions, consumer groups, and environmental organizations, will rectify our deleterious social reality. Moreover, when added to the crucial research and scholastic efforts in various academic settings, to critique our present institutional structures and influences and create new paradigms for their replacement, these cumulative effects will achieve significant ameliorative results.

In my view, at this moment in our life as a nation, neither strategy in and of itself is sufficient to compel the phalanx of offending companies to alter their values and behavior, and become in a moral or behavioral regard exemplary and civically enlightened elements of our society. However, when deployed simultaneously, these efforts will become, in the longer term, a most efficacious approach to the transformation of this country. I view this epic struggle as one might a tactical challenge in a combat environment. These gargantuan entities sit behind barriers congressionally erected, judicially protected, free from substantive, and genuinely inhibiting regulatory restrictions. Thus, what, in my view, is required to mount a sustained, multi-level campaign that unites the previously cited forces of social enlightenment, and the hundreds of organizations that comprise a critical fidelity to very similar normative principles and cultural objectives for this nation. These allies support the continuing attempts to intensify and enlarge my anticipated scope of efforts, in addition to those historic activities which comprise the spectrum of advocacy, protest, electoral involvement, and judicial initiatives.

The moment has long since passed when we should support and patronize massive companies that exist as the incarnation of greed and selfishness, who orchestrate and implement policies and operational behaviors that contravene the moral values which almost all of us embrace, and grievously undermine those democratic principles upon which our nation was founded.

Would you permit your children to play with those who were abusive or bullied them? Would you sustain friendships with neighbors who were guilty of practices unethical or criminal in character? Would you maintain cordial and amicable interactions with institutions or organizations that functioned in a manner concerned solely with benefiting those in their immediate circle while, simultaneously, impacting other facets of the larger community that was harmful? Of course you wouldn't. Most responsible citizens would act to protect their progeny from predators or organic or institutional influences which were negative or injurious.

The great majority of those of us, who discovered their friends were engaged in unethical or illicit actions, would immediately sever those ties. We must abrogate our involvement with these commercial reprobates as well.

We must deprive them of the single most potent weapon in their arsenals, i.e. the financial resources upon which all else is contingent. By diminishing and ultimately discontinuing the flow of revenue that finds its way to their coffers, their capabilities to continue their spectrum of sociopathic behavior shall be permanently interrupted. No longer shall the funds to retain law firms, lobbyists, and consultants in Washington and in state capitols and in major American cities be feasible, and thus shall their power to influence and predetermine legislative outcomes be impaired.

Resources for advertising, marketing, and sales campaigns, particularly with regard to electronic sources of national media, will be constricted, and thus will their sales be negatively impacted.

Discretionary revenues allocated by the boards of directors to repurchase equity in these public corporations will become scarce, and thus will their capacities to increase the value of each share by virtue of decreasing the equity volume to which the public has access plummet. As one quarter of the fiscal year yields to a second and third of increasingly negative news and data about these developments, investors will begin to desert these companies and the downward spiral of the value of each share will accelerate.

As conditions deteriorate further and these companies begin a descent into a status where profits have evaporated and losses are looming ever larger and more frequent, major investor groups shall initiate litigation to oust senior management and/or assume control of the destiny of these commercial enterprises.

Ultimately, should the management of these companies remain adamant in their refusal to transform their modus operandi, they shall forfeit their judicial status as extant "human organisms," and sink into the exceedingly precarious world of one form of bankruptcy or another, frequently never, in any form or structure, to ever reemerge as operating entities. However, another fate could await those who sit astride these huge purveyors of goods and services. As their fortunes deteriorate and the incessantly trumpeted news of their misdeeds, cupidity, and malignant neglect accelerates, this climate of social condemnation might provoke a moral rebirth among board members, and compel then to reform their strategic objectives.

As public awareness of the disastrous effect on the environment which their processes of extraction or manufacture intensifies, those in authority in these institutions may finally become responsive to these major concerns and criticisms, awaken to those responsibilities that are moral, if not legal, in character. Whether this transformation into institutions reflect practices of ethical enterprise is provoked by a moral awakening, or the coercion of an imminent demise, by virtue of our actions I care not; that it occurs whatever the stimulus that is responsible for that metamorphoses, is what is crucial.

In the final analysis, the choice for these organizations is stark and inescapable. Either function in a manner that benefits the entire community, in which your scope of activities operationally resides or perish. The option is yours. However, whatever decision you embrace be aware of this, no longer will so many millions of Americans provide you with the material resources that enable you to augment the chasms of inequality between your corporate colleagues and those of us who are ensnared in the inhospitable precinct of poverty, or exceedingly tenuous membership in the middleclass.

As of this moment, we are committed to the support and patronage of those entities who understand by their pronouncements and behavior, the obligations inherent in the relationship between consumers, and those who would have us acquire what they have provided to the national market place, for sale and consumption.

What we wish to convey to those in positions of administrative prominence in these enterprises is we recognize the supreme irony by our commercial transactions we have been unwitting co-conspirators, and provided you with those resources by which you have acquired your power and wealth and for our current social economic and political predicaments, as well. We hereby serve notice that the era of furnishing, that stream of revenue to perpetuate the continued decrease of our civic efficacy and material circumstances, has come to an irrevocable discontinuation.

At the conclusion of this annual process of both familial and societal assessment, two fundamental continuing responsibilities shall be formulated by you and your family members.

The first addresses what critical alterations of your commercial relationships are required in the ensuing year to expand your universe of ethical commerce, as well as the total cessation of all commercial transactions with companies who appear on the list of Commercial Reprobates.

The second task will be the equally important obligation as a family, to determine what behavioral modifications are necessary to reduce conflict and anxiety within the dynamics of these relationships. A sub-component of the preceding will be to the necessity of implementing the corresponding modifications with individuals and institutions beyond the residence to achieve the fullest expression of your creative talents, personal fulfillment, and contentment with your life.

As you and your loved ones continue to evolve ethically as sentient and caring beings who are equally concerned with the welfare of your fellow citizens, as you are with the well-being of your partner and your nuclear family unit, your joy and serenity will be exponentially augmented.

To those who are reviewing these prescriptions, I am certain among you will emerge the voices of great skepticism and, perhaps, even utter disbelief, American families are either predisposed or capable of these forms of investigation or exploration. Moreover, particularly with regard to the second task which requires a significant degree of objective self-examination, you may very well be of the opinion that this process in order to produce a meaningful and enduring result requires the involvement of a skilled therapist.

During my lifetime, I have benefited greatly from the counsel and analysis of insightful and empathetic therapists. I would be guilty of rank hypocrisy to suggest family members, if they so determine, should not seek participation in a more formally structured process of clinical consultation.

On the contrary, I would heartily endorse their desire to participate in this evaluative activity, for I am of the opinion there are enormous benefits to be realized from these psychological exertions. However, that does not alter my fundamental belief families are frequently capable of identifying those areas of their lives, which cause them suffering and unhappiness, whether the source is within the family or located in an element of the society's normative system, or institutional macro-structures, policies, or cultural or political institutions.

What has convinced me this capability inheres in most of us is my personal experience as a recovering alcoholic. For those of you who are not familiar with Alcoholics Anonymous, the twelve steps, and traditions which undergird and animate much this fellowship is and advocates, I would refer you in particular to what in our spiritual lexicon is the fourth step of our program.

This step states the following: "Made a Searching and Fearless Moral Inventory of Ourselves." What is being requested of the individual recovering alcoholic is to attempt to examine and articulate the nature and content of our ethical sensibilities, our faults, and failings, as well.

For more than seventy-five years of this fellowship's existence, it has been determined in the absence of this activity to pierce the veil of self-deceit, rationalizations, self- justifications, and the atmosphere of denial and self-induced amnesia, and confront the reality of who we have become recovery from this affliction is not possible.

In the individual quest to accomplish the spiritual transformation, which is required at its center, is the continuing collaborative exercise that involves the individual and an efficacy that resides external to this person. It is in some quintessential regard the imperative task of the objective examination of us. I would respectfully suggest this process of examining our modus operandi as human beings, whether afflicted with the disease of alcoholism or not is perhaps the most crucial activity one might undertake. Socrates asserted millennia ago, "The unexamined life is not worth living." Given the contemporary circumstances, it is this mechanism beyond all others required to delineate the fundamental outlines and content of those forces throughout our society, whether they are integral to the family dynamics or external to them responsible for so much that is pathological and inequitable in this nation.

The transcendent fact is so much which is operative in our personal relationships that are negative, damaging, and are sources of frustration, self-loathing, a palpable sense of inadequacy, or paralyzing apprehension, emanates from the ideology extant in this country, also the incapacitating and dehumanizing impacts on our psyches and consciousness the institutional structures that implement this ideology inflict upon virtually all of us. It is incumbent upon us to both investigate and explore these forces and influences which stunt and injure us, and greatly reduce the quotient of happiness in our lives and that of our families.

This process is essentially the reclamation of our fundamental ability to fully implement in our domestic environment and within the larger culture, those values be they religious in origin, or derive from normative perspectives found in Humanist philosophies. The organic implementation of these principles will enable all who are citizens to live in a social atmosphere which nourishes and venerates these moral concerns and priorities.

The principal task for us, as individual citizens, to undertake on this first Saturday in October of each year, commencing in the autumn of 2015, which I am designating as "The First Annual American Assessment Day," is to reaffirm our ethical agendas, and determine how we can improve our familial interactions to mitigate conflict and increase serenity, contentment, and joy. By superimposing this frame of moral reference upon our community, region, and nation, we may construct a schedule of prospective commercial actions for this twelve month period.

The purpose of this exercise is to contribute to the expansion of democratic economic systems and processes and penalize those entities who are responsible for the horrific cultural realities which are extant in the United States and in other areas of the globe. With specific regard to financial institutions, public and private, the hundreds of billions of dollars which have been deposited into these funds are customarily invested in pursuit of profits not derived from projects that reflect a physical reality, such as the construction of public infrastructure office towers, or residential development etc. Nor are they invested, except in infrequent instances, to provide working capital or funds for technological innovations, training for employees, the expansion of product lines, or service capabilities. Rather, they are allotted for mergers and acquisitions, retrieving companies from a public status to one private in character, or expended in the pursuit of arbitrage machinations, credit default instruments, and "dark pools," i.e. a repository of equity holdings either withheld or provided according to computer logarithms, to maximize trading profits.

Profits are derived from the disparities between the prices prospective investors bid to acquire equity in a publicly traded company, and the price which the prospective seller is asking. The continuing objective, of course, is to maximize the profits obtained from these transactions. That these funds may be capable of providing slightly greater returns to investors than other "brick and mortar" projects, and a whole host of other opportunities within the private sector and, without question, within the public bond market, is of little import for two primary reasons.

My initial objection concerns the fact in our domestic or world economy, at any given moment, a finite magnitude of capital exists, and the degree to which these hundreds of billions of dollars are apportioned to the primary activities which comprise the investment portfolio of most hedge funds, do these resources become unavailable for any other investment purpose.

These profits usually find their way into the accounts of individuals and institutions of extraordinary net worth who are not predisposed to funnel these funds into projects that create jobs, improve communities, or mitigate unemployment, and this reluctance becomes a principal factor in the perpetuation of our economic plight and social devastation. Moreover, to compound this deprivation of capital for projects that would benefit so many of our citizens, the profits these forms of investment produce are taxed at rates when, compared to the tax burdens which wage earners are required to pay to the I.R.S. etc., are significantly lower. In addition, because Congress has historically acquiesced to the desire of lobbyists representing these titans of industry, substantial loopholes in this category of legislation exists and, as a result their obligations are reduced still further, and, in some instances, entirely eliminated.

Whatever exceedingly modest gains these institutions produce in the return on these hedge fund investments, when compared to more traditional investment opportunities, is totally eclipsed by their deployment in financial adventures that benefit few who have already amassed enormous material resources.

It is these investments into arcane fiscal propositions deprive our nation of a source of wealth that contains the potential were it committed appropriately, to achieve great rewards for those whose foothold in the middleclass is becoming ever more tenuous, as well as the poor.

On an annual basis, I shall dispatch to these private capital firms a questionnaire that seeks information regarding the considerations which appear previously, as well as other inquiries that are relevant.

My expectation is some firms shall be responsive, but many may not. Their cooperation will be noted, as will their lack of transparency should they refuse to furnish this data. Beyond these entities, there are numerous sources of information to which we have access, business publications, such as *The Wall Street Journal*, U.S. Chamber of Commerce periodicals, *The National Association of Manufacturers* and their flow of press releases, and *Forbes* and *Fortune Magazines*, to cite the most prominent of those within the realm of print media.

In the realm of electronic media, MSNBC, and other cable channels, the business segments of major networks news programs, and other media outlets and programs focusing on the intermittent commingling and disentanglement of companies, as well as their contractual relationships.

Other news sources release statistics which reflect the ebb and flow of revenue and profitability streams, the trajectories of the value of the equity shares in these firms, and other significant developments that reflect their activities. Investigative journalists will also be consulted. Thus, through a series of methods and modalities will it be in possible to provide to the American consumer a portrait of their investments, their domestic and international involvements, and most crucially when their funds are deployed in the service of mergers and acquisitions, and/or converting public companies into private entities.

In addition, we shall publicize the impact of these completed transactions on such considerations as compensation for the average employee, access by these individuals to stock options or equity accumulations, the presence of employees on the board of directors, and other salient factors. Moreover, we shall also report whether or not their manufacturing and/or service processes support a sustainable economy, and finally, the level of participation these newly minted entities commit, to the mitigation of economic and social challenges extant in their respective communities.

It is the forgoing standards of measurement in the new calculus of American commerce to which major private sector firms shall be held accountable, of equal importance in a political context, to the requirement to provide products and services of quality priced competitively, and whose business practices vis-a-vis the consumer and all others reflect an ethical content.

Yes, the continued expectation these institutions shall be managed in a cost-effective manner and be committed to profitable operations, as well as the maintenance of a fiduciary responsibility to shareholders and other investors, will not be rescinded. However, what must change if these entities wish to remain viable the era in American capitalism in which these organizations were legally mandated to maximize profits, irrespective of the costs and damage to other sectors of this nation and its citizens, this morally benighted perspective must be rejected. Moreover, their behavior will be evaluated by a reassertion of the timeless moral instructions contained in our theologies and within our Humanistic normative constraints, and thus will assume the first priority and most crucial index of analysis, by which we judge all commercial behavior.

From this moment on in our history, these enterprises will be required to provide a favorable response to this interrogatory: "Beyond the commercial practices in which you engage in the American marketplace, is your presence and activity in this society responsible for its improvement and evolution regarding both ethical principles and democratic realities?"

Should you be evaluated by this standard and are found wanting, our citizens will discontinue their patronage, and support instead those entities who proudly declare and may be empirically confirmed, to be functioning m in that modus operandi.

The Annual Logistics of Evaluating
Those Who Reflect Ethical Commerce Business Practices
and Those Who Comprise the Category of Commercial Reprobates

It is our intent, on an annual basis, to explore and examine the two realms and the entities that comprise them that appear above. Among the principal sources of information we shall consult beyond the company's websites, are other entries that appear in tandem with and predate and antedate, the data the company is providing to the public about their operations.

Are there instances where various practices of this organization are deemed innovative and support aspects of an ethical commerce? Of what are they comprised? The impact on employees, shareholders, the community in which they are situated, as well as the quality of the products and services they offer to the consuming public, do these practices yield? We shall highlight the awards which are bestowed upon various companies by Schools of Entrepreneurialism, and programs within the academy beneath the umbrella of Social Enterprise.

The kudos of such publications as Inc. and their yearly compendium of those one hundred companies most successful by standards of measurement infinitely more comprehensive than a substantial enhancement of their streams of revenue and profitability will be featured.

Other business publications, and those associations that represent the small business owner, as well as organizations emerging and evolving into medium commercial enterprises, institutes, centers of research, economic and policy as well as, think tanks that focus on those concerns. They will have their most significant reports prominently displayed on our website. In addition, those facts that may be gleaned from stories in the world of electronic media be they positive or negative in substance about these companies will be presented, as well as judicial decisions that emanate from state and federal jurisdictions impact these enterprises.

News stories which focus on political decisions, particularly at the national and international level regarding taxation policy, federal tax code exemptions, tax forgiveness mergers and acquisitions, the environmental impacts of multinational corporations, and central considerations of sustainable economic activity, shall be unfailingly communicated to our readers.

An unrelenting spotlight will illuminate the activities of lobbyists and their client rosters within the congressional, and regulatory realms, and the White House. It will transmit our citizens' information about those campaigns that are attempts to stimulate public sentiment regarding various policies and pending legislation, shall also be assessed and included in these summaries.

As a result of these continuous efforts to provide a comprehensive and particularistic stream of information to the American public, those commercial enterprises that should be supported commercially and expand to become a regional, national, or international presence, in the global marketplace, will assume center stage as the result of our accolades.

Simultaneously, those entities engaging in business practices destructive of numerous crucial elements of our society and politics they should be deprived of all revenues, and endorsements, shall bask in the notoriety they richly deserve. Thus, in this state of commercial ostracism they will either reform their modus operandi or, in a continuing posture of intransigence, find their ignominious pathway to a state of bankruptcy and, in their insolvency, sink beneath the waves of viability.

Their example will be a testament to others who refuse to abandon this trio of greed, inimical social impacts, and the attenuation of our nation's political process that exists to represent the interests of the majority of citizens, and not the priorities of the miniscule universe of billionaires, as to the cruel and unforgiving economic fate that awaits them in their recalcitrance.

Beyond the annual consultation, with these troves of data which it is my fervent hope ever greater numbers of Americans will consult, on the first Saturday of October commencing in the autumn of 2015, i.e. "The First Annual American Assessment Day," to determine which commercial entities should be patronized and which should be rejected as unworthy of continued support.

It is my hope our citizens shall devote in addition one hour a week to this website, so they may remain abreast of those developments that occur regarding their commercial behavior.

Our status reports may very well reflect the fact additional companies, as the result of actions ethically objectionable, and/or politically deleterious to various elements of our society, have been placed with other miscreants on the list of "Commercial Reprobates."

This process of evaluation will be fluid, dynamic, and unceasing, in its attempt to provide our citizens with the most current information possible about these entities, their involvements, and institutional behavior. Moreover, as those who function ethically are rewarded for these practices by increased revenues and profitability, and expand from local communities to a regional or national presence, it will be possible for those in the areas of this nation in which they establish commercial outlets, to join with countless others in patronizing these enterprises.

It is this strategy that ultimately will transform this nation, for as ethical commerce increases and the reform, or cessation of operations of those who benefit from the current social and political circumstances are diminished, the afflictions of great inequality, a deteriorating political participation by significant numbers of those who are alienated by their impotency, will recede.

What replaces the preceding will be an infinitely more egalitarian civic atmosphere in which contentment, personal creative expression, and equitable institutional arrangements will commingle, to introduce America into an unprecedented era of social justice and individual moral development? A utopia? Of course not. A civic culture bereft of conflict and disagreement about much that transpires in the United States? Absolutely not. However, in some fundamental regard the qualitative nature of these contentious issues and divisive forces will not reach into the very foundation of our democracy, and thus will these opposing viewpoints be infinitely more amenable to political resolution.

The contemporary reality is divisive and acrimonious an imminent period of great social unrest looms largely, and ultimately, should the desires of so many of our citizens remain ignored or dismissed, the possibility of a violent expression of those discontents could imperil our continuation as a society. To add these instruments of assisting ethical commerce and penalizing sources of immoral and punitive activity in the realm of business organizations, shall be a most powerful tool in accompanying the millions of our citizens who are engaged in the entire spectrum of activity political, intellectual, environmental, of those efforts to remediate our social ills.

To those who are already engaged in these struggles to transform this nation through the efforts of nonprofit, for-profit, not-for-profit, public instrumentalities, and combinations and permutations of the preceding categories of exertion, I commend you for your efforts, and exhort you to continue the allocation of your energy and intelligence to these causes.

What I am advocating in addition to these undertakings is a powerful complement to your participation in these campaigns to achieve social justice, i.e. rewarding the growth of ethical commerce and discontinuing all financial involvement with companies or corporations who are responsible for the nation's reprehensible status quo.

To abrogate entirely and irrevocably the financial resources that currently flow to these entities is the most immediate and effective manner of conveying our outrage and indignation, about the suffering of our middleclass and those who reside in the dungeons of poverty. In too many tragic instances, it is the sole instrument those at the apogee of these organizations will be chastened and morally disciplined, or by their recalcitrance, cease to exist.

The dismantling of this "architecture of social dysfunction and oppressive inequality" will inaugurate a resurrection in this nation, of those religious principles and political commitments to our citizens who have been impoverished and deprived of their vigor and influence, for more than four decades.

This reinvigoration is long past due and it is the single most important task to which we must address ourselves if we wish to resuscitate our democracy and enjoy a life of personal meaning and fulfillment. From this process of rejuvenation, will there also be derived a collective comprehension and implementation of those imperative moral precepts that will finally redeem a culture which the progressive forces in our nation have been striving to bring into being, since the inception of this nation. Let us wait no longer. Let us redouble our efforts and remain committed until the transformation of America has been successfully concluded!